THE MURAL—AN AUTHENTIC REPRODUCTION OF THE WILDERNESS CAPITAL DURING LINCOLN'S
LAWMAKING PERIOD

Vandalia: Wilderness Capital of Lincoln's Land

by

MARY BURTSCHI

Drawings by

Josephine Burtschi

Huston-Patterson Corporation   •   Decatur

Printed by

Huston-Patterson Corporation
Decatur, Illinois

10

PREFACE

There has been in recent years a number of requests for a readable history of Vandalia for the purpose of guiding visitors through the old capital of Illinois. The first request came from Miss Carrie Darner, a dedicated public school teacher whose inspiration greatly furthered this undertaking. The author has devoted seven years in preparation of this work and has found a far greater amount of material written about the capital period than anticipated and as a result has taken the privilege of selecting material rather than making an attempt to write a complete history. The author has tried to communicate the spirit that has gone into achieving a democratic government on the prairie wilderness. Americans, it is greatly hoped, will investigate for themselves the great activity displayed in Vandalia by these early patriots in response to the needs, aspirations, and hopes of the early pioneers.

There will be more detailed, more scholarly, and more impressive histories written about this old town, but it is fervently hoped that the authors of them will find substantial and useful information in this book. The primary endeavor of this account is to present material that will serve to promote interest and to help visitors to learn about the colonization, the great personalities, historic buildings, and numerous items left in the town. If the reader falls under the enchantment of these personalities and events, the author will be highly pleased. If the student of history and literature finds that this work possesses a vital interest to him, the author will be repaid for her many hours of toil.

TABLE OF CONTENTS

ILLUSTRATIONS

This book is affectionately dedicated to the memory of the author's father, Joseph Charles Burtschi, the historian who first inspired her interest in early Vandalia chronicles.

INTRODUCTION

Travelers along the old National Road, which has been converted (it does not, however, follow the exact route) into the modern Interstate 70, are assured a reward by their inquiry into the history of Vandalia, Illinois. This frontier home of gallant settlers of the early West is a commonly unknown aspect of American life. It is rich in historical interest that is stimulating to thought because it is so worth investigating and so rewarding to the visitor who makes the effort to inquire. Vandalia sits securely and confidently on the west bank of the Kaskaskia (the nomenclature of the river reflects its Indian history), certain of capturing the attention and interest of American travelers.

In 1819 Vandalia offered an attractive region—rolling hills, magnificent timber, spring water, and an abundance of wildflowers and flowering trees—to Americans and Europeans who wanted a new life. The woodlands and water to a certain extent still abound with wild-life. This area is still one of beauty during spring, summer, and autumn.

The National Road, commonly called the Cumberland Road in this locality, leads visitors to Vandalia to tread the streets, and to see the frontier buildings and the sites which notable American patriots like Abraham Lincoln, Stephen Douglas, Edward Coles, James Hall, Morris Birkbeck, Peter Cartwright, John Mason Peck, Orville Hickman Browning, James W. Berry, Edward Dickinson Baker, Sidney Breese, Alexander Pope Field, and Robert Blackwell knew so well. Looking into a past age will permit the traveler to leave Vandalia with a better understanding of the traditions and culture of the early West, but one who rushes through Illinois on Interstate 70 without turning off on the old National Road will pass charms to satisfy the lover of natural beauty and the American interested in his historic past.

This old town is probably the only place in the world that does not tend to apotheosize the great Abraham Lincoln, who spent five legislative sessions from 1834-1839 in the capital as a lawmaker. It was through his vigorous efforts that Vandalia lost its identification as the active capital of Illinois. The colorful and dramatic record included in this book stretches from the first year of settlement in 1819 to the removal of the capital in 1839. But without the memory of the remarkable Lincoln the old town would doubtfully capture the attention of the traveler. When he stops to see the town where Lincoln served as a lawmaker, he then learns the compelling story of Vandalia.

COLONIZATION OF
THE EARLY CAPITAL

This is a story of a pioneer village wrought out of a forest and born to be the capital of the new state of Illinois. It is a story of beginnings which has the freshness and vigor of youth in quest of the ideal of democracy. The early settlement of Vandalia was created in 1819 for the sole purpose of carrying on a new kind of political freedom which the Eastern colonists had won. Establishing democratic seats of government in the West normally followed the winning of political freedom in the East. Men interested in the future of America—men from the social extremes of Eastern colleges and rough frontier—met in an atmosphere of compromise. They had certain ideas in common, namely, belief in the democratic ideal and faith in the future.

The policies and principles shaped here from 1820-1839 were essentially American in character; therefore it is reasonable to assume that the early settlement of Vandalia lends itself to a national interest. Furthermore, the outstanding American statesman who came upon this political scene was Abraham Lincoln. For that reason alone Vandalia merits interest. Much was accomplished here to prevent slavery in the infant state. Early before Lincoln appeared in Vandalia, freedom was a conception that the early settlers cherished and fought for to become a reality.

When those who established the capital penetrated this area, Indians were not permanent residents. There was no burning of farms or unwarranted attacks upon people. After 1819 no incident has been recorded concerning savage tribes who became troublesome in this particular area. The only mention of Indians is the peaceful, docile Kickapoos who came during the hunting season to the banks of the Kaskaskia.

General Anthony Wayne's successes lessened Indian wars in the Midwest during Washington's administration, making this region safer for white settlers. The destruction of the buffalo herd which furnished the tribes much of their food, skins for tepees, clothing, and strings for their bows caused the failure of Indians to compete with the forces of the United States Army.

Buffalo in 1819 had disappeared although the prairies had been their natural habitat. Even during capital days the settlers spoke of the high prairie grass which reached to their shoulders. The buffalo ate of this grass, fattening themselves for the kill by the Indians in the autumn. When the buffalo herd assembled in great numbers, the red men set fire to the grass which encircled the animals. Only one pass was left for the buffalo to avoid the fire. The Indians stationed themselves at this passage, killing the animals with their bows and arrows as they attempted to escape the burning grass.

A digression from the Indian at this point might serve to show the great danger of prairie fires with which the settlers had to contend. One summer about four years after the Hanover Colony had come to Vandalia, Christian Yerker with several companions was cutting the tall prairie grass two miles west of town when it suddenly caught fire. Yerker attempted to save his hay, but in his effort he was unable to seek escape from the fire that crackled around him. Frantic and horror-stricken, his companions failed to save him from perishing in the intense heat.[1]

To some readers the Kickapoo tribe may be unfamiliar. It originally occupied a part of Wisconsin but moved into Illinois about 1765. At this time the Kickapoos abandoned their agricultural life and became nomads, many moving into Illinois territory. In 1819 they ceded their lands in central Illinois to the United States. No doubt the reason that the tribe remained here after 1819 was that Kennekuk (also spelled *Kanakuk*), the chief, avoided trouble with the government by exhorting his people to live peaceably with the white man by obeying his laws and refraining from the use of alcohol. Under his command the Kickapoos lived for many years in Illinois. Half the tribe, however, moved into Mexico when the lands were ceded while the other portion remaind in this state. The Kickapoos felt it unwise to go to their assigned reservation in Missouri—a land occupied by their enemy the Osage.

It has been related by early settlers that the Kickapoos had a village one hundred miles north of Vandalia and that much of Fayette

County was used as their hunting grounds. A small village stood where the Pennsylvania Railroad crosses Owl Creek and another on the river bluff about two miles south of Vandalia. The Kickapoos often moved their settlements up and down the Kaskaskia River. During the early capital years the Kickapoos returned each autumn in a group of two to three hundred spending about six weeks hunting and fishing. Since they were friendly, the white settlers were not concerned about their presence.

However, in 1790 reports indicate "when surveyors moved up the Kaskaskia River to its source, they were attacked by the Kickapoo who resided in the prairies of north-central Illinois."[2] Although the settlers in Vandalia dwelt in safety far removed from any conflict with the Indian in 1819, the red man presented a problem in other parts of the state. In Coles County, Indians resented the encroachment of white settlers to such an extent that there existed no permanent settlement prior to 1820. Furthermore, in northern Illinois forts were constructed because of constant threat of Indian attacks.

Since the Indian in this area was not troublesome, pioneers moved into the Vandalia environs several years before the town existed. It would be impossible to mention all the families who settled near Vandalia prior to the time it was founded as the capital. Guy Beck, a blacksmith from Kentucky, and his wife came to Illinois in 1809, settling in St. Clair County. It was in 1815 after he had served in the War of 1812 that he settled a tract of land north of Vandalia and built a cabin on the banks of a creek that bears his name. Hunting and fishing were good enough for a livelihood at this time, and apparently he preferred that to the toilsome work of farming. Especially difficult was plowing the prairie. Guy Beck operated a small blacksmith shop at his home to which the neighbors brought their farm implements to be repaired.[3] Guy Beck and his wife have been credited with being the first settlers of Fayette County, and the residents of Ramsey, the nearest town to the Beck acreage, take pride in this fact. In 1818 another family early known for its fine community spirit was Jeremiah Evans, his wife, and two sons, John and Akin, who emigrated from Virginia and settled south of Vandalia. Although Evans built a blacksmith shop in 1821 for his private use, he assisted neighbors by mending their wagons and implements or by sharpening their plows

3

for which he made no charge. The Beck and Evans families are mentioned since their activities have a certain historical significance in this area.

Illinois was admitted into the Union as a sovereign state in 1818. Five commissioners, Samuel Whiteside, Levi Compton, William Alexander, Thomas Cox, and Guy Smith were appointed by the General Assembly in Kaskaskia, the former territorial capital, to provide for laying out a town to be the state capital. Section Two of the act to remove the seat of government from Kaskaskia stipulated that the land was to be situated "on the Kaskaskia river, and was near as may be east of the third principal meridian on said river." The following year the commissioners selected the site of Vandalia to be the seat of government for twenty years. From the chronicles of past time and from oral repetition an incident that has been regarded by fellow-historians as authentic must be noted. It is doubtful that Finney Preston, an Olney lawyer, imposed any fabrication of his own. During the 1870's Robert Ross learned from Preston that one of the five commissioners had told him that when the commissioners were making their way along the west bank of the Kaskaskia River to select "a suitable site whereon to fix the seat of government of this state," a member of the group shot a deer that fell at the trunk of a large white oak tree which stood on the spot where the Statehouse now stands. The men dressed the deer, cooked a portion of it, and while eating it, they made the decision that the capitol should be erected on the precise spot where the deer had fallen. The incident whether legendary or true is a part of the material that makes Vandalia's history so colorful.

William C. Greenup, along with Beal Greenup and John McCollum, was appointed to survey the unbroken wilderness on the bluff overlooking the Kaskaskia River. Greenup was instructed to reserve one square or block upon which the permanent capitol should be erected. The surveyors completed the assignment July, 1819. Since the energies of the settlers were constantly directed to the land, the transit which Greenup used is a cherished item retained by the Vandalia people.

At this point it might be well to discuss the derivation of the name *Vandalia* which has been uncertain for these many years. George W.

Brown recalled to mind a conversation between Colonel Greenup and Brown's father in which the surveyor explained the origin of the name *Vandalia*. When Greenup was surveying and platting the village, someone made the suggestion that it be called *van*, an abbreviation of the word *vanguard*, which meant the front of an advancing body composed of individuals. In military formation a van was the leading unit; such a name would indicate the front of any movement, and the phrase "a nation in the van of progress" was commonly used. Another person suggested the term *dalia* since the Anglo-Saxon word *dale* means a river valley between hills or high land. The topography consists of low-lying tracts among vales or dales. Greenup informed Brown that he connected the two names, signifying a leading unit in the progress of a nation in a place of dales. The fact that Greenup was the surveyor gives weight to this derivation. Since Brown, a cashier of the National Bank of Vandalia and a man of good reputation, recorded the telling of the incident, it is a probable solution to the naming of Vandalia. Charles F. Houston, grandson of Augustus Synder of the Ernst Colony, supports Brown's integrity and clarity of memory, confirming that such an incident occurred if Mr. Brown stated it. Robert Ross, editor of *Historical Souvenir of Vandalia, Illinois* (1904), also maintains that such a solution of the origin of the name is reasonable.

The Vandalia Colony, a land-grant scheme originating in England between 1767 and 1776, the charter of which was nullified by the outbreak of the Revolution, is another possible derivation. Since the royal charter extended to the area of Vandalia, it is possible the capital was named for that colony. The derivation continues to be a mooted point principally concerning the above explanations.

Another theory expounded in the past was that a wag named the town *Vandalia* since a tribe of Indians called Vandals inhabited this area. History does not record a tribe by that name in Illinois. Furthermore, if the wag intended to make light of the town by applying a name reminiscent of people who destroyed monuments of art and culture as did the Vandals, who sacked Rome in the fifth century, it is quite improbable that the early settlers would select such an offensive name for the capital. Certainly that theory can be easily exploded as witness the fourth section of the act for the removal of the seat of government of the state of Illinois: "and the state commissioners shall have the right to give to the said town some proper and appropriate name as they may agree upon." Undoubtedly these men would not have permitted a wag to name the town attaching such a meaning.

The name *Vandalia* was mentioned in the act approving and confirming the proceedings of these commissioners as witness the first section of the act: "and the said town of Vandalia, laid out by the said commissioners on part of said four sections, is hereby declared to be the permanent seat of government of the state of Illinois for twenty years from and after the first Monday of December, 1820."

The primitive little capital bustled with activity when the first legislative session was held in December. The General Assembly in February, 1821, approved the appointment of William L. D. Ewing, Thomas Cox, James Duncan, Robert McLaughlin, Ferdinard Ernst, John Warnock, and Joshua Barnes, trustees to the town of Vandalia, to erect a bridge across the Kaskaskia and construct a road over the bottom east of the river to the highlands, to paint the Statehouse, to prevent horse-racing in the streets and lanes, to impose fines for their breaches of ordinances, to prevent any waste of timber on the four sections of land granted for the seat of government, and to perform various other duties for the welfare of the town.

Although much can be gained from the legislative records, Vandalia is not without personal accounts written by the colonists. Frederick Hollman's *Autobiography*, a simple, straightforward account covering the years 1819-1827, remains the most trustworthy personal chronicle of the early months of Vandalia's infancy when a small group of colonists from Hanover, Germany, under the leadership of Ferdinand Ernst, struggled to establish a culture in the wilderness of Illinois. Such a record of personal experiences is a first-hand study of pioneer life on the prairies. Hollman, who voluntarily abandoned position, comfort, and friends, seems to avoid telling the privations of life in the early days of the Ernst Colony. Instead he records his experiences in securing supplies, hiring men to erect buildings, and learning the English language. No doubt he had been trained to admire courage, and the hard conditions gave him an opportunity to exercise his ingenuity. Or perhaps he shared Morris

Birkbeck's viewpoint. In the preface of Birkbeck's book *Letters from Illinois* (1818) the Britisher admonishes the man who comes to the wilderness and lets his mind dwell on the faults and "overlooks the present good."

When Ferdinand Ernst, a well-educated German of substantial financial means, contemplated founding a colony in America, he requested the moral support of Frederick Hollman. That is precisely what he received. It is fortunate that these two gentlemen had crossed each other's paths earlier in Germany. During the period of three years (1807-1810) when Hollman was attending an agricultural college in Germany, he resided with the Ferdinand Ernst family. At the end of his instruction Hollman served as superintendent of a large domain at Gutenstadt where he was satisfied with both the position and the salary. However, when he met Ernst in 1819 in the city of Hildesheim, Ernst told him that he had sold all his possessions for $45,000 and intended to found a colony in the new world on the banks of the Kaskaskia in the infant state of Illinois. Ernst proposed that Hollman join him in this enterprise and was successful in persuading him to forsake his distinguished position as superintendent and to emigrate to America.

At Bremen on March 17, 1819, the two men sailed for America and arrived in Baltimore on June 15, 1819. When they came to Vandalia, they found a dense wilderness of mammoth oak, graceful walnuts, hickories, and ash. Ernst recorded: "How difficult it was at that time to penetrate the dense forest which embraces the entire circuit of the future city." [4] The promoter could visualize the disappearance of these huge trees and in their place buildings hewn out of the timber. Frantz, a servant who accompanied them, remained with Frederick Hollman to construct houses for the German colonists who would arrive within the next year with Ernst.

Certainly Hollman, a man of European civilization, secured a broader comprehension of human existence in this wilderness; although he does not mention life's struggles and failures, he must have realized them keenly the year he was preparing with Frantz to make ready the capital for human occupation. On the outskirts of the capital there lived hunters who supported themselves and their families by killing deer and planting corn. After overcoming the

7

difficulty of communicating in the English language with hunters and squatters whom he met, he managed to carry out Ernst's orders to build. Hollman's first shelter consisted of a framework of poles covered with brush. He found enough rough men to penetrate the thickets of the river bottom and the forest to secure timber. An old squatter erected for him the first log cabin which measured sixteen by fourteen feet. The most incredible fact that confronts the modern reader in terms of value is that Hollman and his chopper selected the finest walnut trees from which to saw boards to build log cabins.

Later emigrants, making their way to Vandalia, soon were building primitive habitations within the boundary of the capital. The hunters brought to the frontier market deer skins and venison hams. A new world it was to Hollman—log cabins, grassy plains interspersed with groves and trees, deer and wolves roaming through the settlement, old trappers, dressed in buckskin breeches, coon-skin caps, and moccasins, and carrying powder horns, women plainly dressed in calico and sunbonnets, and a rabble that is found in all frontier towns.

One would be naive indeed to presume that scoundrels, robbers, and murderers were not a part of an early frontier town. Although Hollman seldom directs attention to lurid tales of outlaws in his *Autobiography*, he does speak of the gang of robbers and counterfeiters who operated between Vincennes and the Mississippi River. When the Ernst Colony arrived by riverboat at Shawneetown, Hollman's men with a number of ox teams met them to bring them and their possessions to Vandalia. The household utensils and wearing apparel of the colonists were packed in large German chests —two of which are still in existence. Hollman's description of them is quite articulate—"heavy, unwieldly German emigrants' chests."[5] Robbers attacked the wagon train, hopped aboard the wagons, and ransacked the trunks expecting to find valuable cargo. Instead they found items like "iron pots, rusty kettles, old axes, worthless chains, crockery ware, bedding, wearing apparel, etc.,"[6] Hollman records. Angry to find such worthless items, they scattered the contents in every direction on the road and departed leaving the teamsters to gather the things.

So Hollman records little about crimes or other offensive realities. He was too busy turning his energy to building a community worthy of being called a seat of government to be daunted by the biting cold, the labor of cutting firewood, or the primitive methods of seeking food. Instead he records that game was so plentiful it was "astonishing." Bears, elks, deer, turkeys, pheasants, geese, duck, and fish were in the wilderness for the effort. Hollman does remark that his account sounds much like "a fabulous romance," but it is "truthful." [7]

Due to Hollman's energy and fidelity to purpose there were suitable accommodations for the members when the Illinois Legislature met in 1820. It had been in session for four weeks when the strains of "Hail Columbia" sounded through the air. A lively German band was playing the patriotic tune as a wagon train entered the new capital. Ernst's colony was arriving from Hanover. The little band, cheering the hearts of all, played the tune on the way to the statehouse. About sixty men, women, and children, some on foot and some in wagons, were following. Indeed the sight of his countrymen and the music of the band gladdened Hollman's heart and removed any burdens that his year of toil had caused. He actually wept with joy. Hollman suggested to the colonists that they give three hurrahs for the state of Illinois and three for the legislators. Excitement was intense. Then the band made its way to Ernst's home playing the tune of "Yankee Doodle." [8] Such excitation filled the air as the Hanover Colony made its entrance. What other newly organized settlement could boast of such an impressive show of love for an adopted country?

Colonies in the new world were usually founded for commercial reasons by an organization which served a financial purpose. Ernst must not have had any dreams of securing profits from the colonization. He was enthusiastic, however, about the advantages of agriculture when he made his first visit to this area in 1818. He collected various samples of grasses and cereals, and after his return to Germany he published a pamphlet concerning the superior opportunities for agricultural pursuits in Illinois. Notwithstanding this fact, there seems to be only one motive for the colonists whom he persuaded to come: a romantic adventure in the wilderness that would result in a successful settlement for a new seat of government. Such was their hope, but during the years 1824-1825 disease took many colonists and one by one death resulted. When the illness proved fatal to Ernst, some of the surviving colonists left Vandalia, and the hopeful colony became a "sad delusion" as Hollman expressed it. Whatever were their reasons for coming to the wilderness capital, the colonists must have had great courage to cross the three thousand miles of ocean, knowing that hard conditions would exist.

At the very founding of the town, Ernst, Smith, and Hollman, all university men, served to direct attention to intellectual pursuits and amenities of life. It cannot be said, however, that the majority of Hanover colonists played a significant role in developing culture. The Berrys, McLaughlins, and Blackwells, who came from Kaskaskia in 1819, contributed a substantial influence to the elevated tone of capital society and became prominent in the affairs of the state. These families who continued to reside in Vandalia after the removal of the capital provided an intellectual stimulus and an enriched cultural life for the town. The very books that they left to the later residents of Vandalia indicate that they had received stimulation of mind and inspiration from the writings of the immortals. The custom of calling, acknowledging courtesies by notes, and other amenities persisted into the twentieth century in Vandalia. The Kaskaskia group combined their efforts in a rugged environment to open up a new world of culture on the frontier.

Likewise, the legislators and state officers contributed a commendable portion of culture to the capital. The college-trained men like Elias Kent Kane, Sidney Breese, Edward Coles, and others were not only law-abiding, but they offered an intellectual strength and social refinement that settlers of other localities rarely possessed. Immigrants who poured into the new state were usually those who lived by the ax and rifle. The lawmakers coming to a little clearing in the wilderness were equally amazed at both the living quarters and type of intelligent people who inhabited the new settlement. Vandalia, however, was not without its tough and lawless element who disappeared into the forest to escape punishment for crime nor were drunkards an uncommon sight. On the other hand, the town was populated with more of the well-bred and literate than were most new settlements. The caliber of people who lived in early Vandalia received praise from Robert Ross in his *Souvenir* of 1904: "Taken

10

together a more cultured, refined and intelligent group of people were never congregated in as small a place as Vandalia at that time." [9]

Illinois need not be ashamed of her early culture. Some historians would have readers believe, for example, that the hard conditions of life discouraged intellectual pursuits and refinement of manners. It was in 1824 that the distinguished Morris Birkbeck managed the affairs of state with the discretion and zeal of an English statesman. Furthermore, he did an inestimable service to the state when he defended democracy and freedom, basing his arguments on the political philosophies of Locke and Jefferson in his anti-slavery pamphlets and newspaper articles written in clear, forceful English. Thirteen years later Abraham Lincoln's prepared protest against slavery, a specific document spread on the *House Journal*, was written in clear, precise prose on an issue that attained national prominence.

It was in 1827 when James Hall appeared that a lasting literary expression was given to this life. Hall found enchantment in this world of nature and frontier environment; his poetry and prose are full of the happy discovery of this new world of Illinois. Certainly James Berry's art is notable for its achievement. One has only to view his oil portraits of Governor Bond, the McLaughlins, Washington, and Lafayette to realize his talent despite the fact that he is not widely known. The Vandalia newspaper, for example, in 1827 included a reference to James Fenimore Cooper's new novel *The Prairie; a Tale*. It was apparent that the editor knew the author had embodied action, adventure, and vivid description in his previous novel *The Pioneers*. Even in the midst of physical activity the colonists themselves recorded material. Frederick Hollman was no stylist in the literary sense of the word, but he wrote with a clarity and cogency that keeps alive the early days of the settlement.

The interest in music is noteworthy among the colonists who were not too busy to provide their own entertainment during the evenings. It must have been strange to hear the tender strains of Hayden, Mozart, Beethoven, and Handel sounding over the prairies. Perhaps the music of these composers was not presented by an efficient corps of performers, but the fact that it prevailed shows a discerning and resourceful group who enjoyed the art. Handel's message of music

11

must have been both solace and joy to the Hanover emigrants. On the other hand, it must have called into being feelings of homesickness during the long winter evenings amidst the blustery prairie winds. Hollman records the fact that the colonists, possessing some degree of talent, applied themselves to music:

> We performed with considerable ease the compositions of Handel, Beethoven, Mozart, and Hayden. It was in such refined company and such association that I had passed my early life in Germany and it was like surroundings that I passed a number of years in Vandalia after the arrival of Mr. Ernst and his friends.[10]

The Ernst group played the music of their own Handel, for it was in Hanover from where the Ernst Colony came that Handel was appointed court conductor. The interest in Handel still lives on in Vandalia. During the yuletide season the high school students sing *The Messiah*, Handel's greatest oratorio, and have presented the Christmas portions since 1944. The established custom of standing when the singers begin the "Hallelujah Chorus" and remain standing during its rendition is followed by the Vandalia audience. Although it is a custom followed by all audiences at the performances of *The Messiah*, it is a bit of tradition to continue the old custom first started by George II in London. On a winter afternoon in December of each year Handel's music sounds again over the prairies. It brings Vandalians a happiness that the first colonists must have felt when they applied themselves to Handel's expressive compositions.

But such application by the early colonists was one of the few bright spots in their lives. Indeed the colonization of the capital was a heavy task. The problems of obtaining food and fuel for the remorseless winters, the transportation inconveniences, and the ravages of disease were not conducive to an ordered life which the colonists had left in Hanover. But the early settlers who wrote to encourage newcomers to the territory showed a passionate enthusiasm for the adventurous life that could be turned into a better one for the individual who looked for political and social equality.

COLONIZATION OF THE CAPITAL
1. Brink, McDonough & Co., History of Fayette County, Illinois (Philadelphia, 1878), p. 26
2. Wayne C. Temple, Indian Villages of the Illinois Country: Historic Tribes (Springfield, 1958), p. 163
3. Brink, McDonough & Co., op. cit., p. 25
4. Joseph C. Burtschi, Documentary History of Vandalia, Illinois (Decatur, 1954), p. 25
5. Ibid., p. 34
6. Ibid., p. 35
7. Vandalia Historical Society, Hollman MSS.
8. Ibid.
9. Robert W. Ross (ed.), Historical Souvenir of Vandalia, Illinois (Effingham, 1904), p. 33
10. Burtschi, op., cit., p. 34

SEVEN GOVERNORS

In Vandalia Americans met on a common ground and coped with difficulties, ever mindful of having their rights as free men respected. Problems germane to the democratic life and society needed solving. The seven governors whom the pioneers elected contributed their intellect, energy, and support to the advancement of democratic ideals. A biographical sketch of each governor in this chapter will give the reader an idea of the tasks at which these men labored so that Americans might profit in their own personal lives from this service to the state. Besides a feverish political activity, there was a social and intellectual life in which these governors found themselves beyond all precedent in the infancy of a frontier town.

SHADRACH BOND (1818-1822)

The first man to bear the title governor of Illinois was Shadrach Bond (1773-1832). In 1791 he left his family in Baltimore County, Maryland, to join his uncle who had settled near Kaskaskia, Illinois, on the Mississippi River. While he devoted his time to farming on the American Bottom, he attempted to acquire knowledge that would be useful to him during life. He was elected in 1806 to the territorial legislature. Shadrach Bond, whose mind had the force and self-discipline to learn without formal training, took up the responsibilities of political life on the Western frontier. His countrymen were entering a new age in which great changes were pending in government. In 1812 he was the first delegate to Congress from the Illinois territory. Bond also served as captain in the War of 1812. In 1814 he received an appointment to settle land claims in the southern part of Illinois. An oil portrait of Bond as he appeared when a captain in the War of 1812 attests to the fact that his mein was distinguished and his appearance commanding. Along with his interest in improving his intellect and with his dignified bearing he exerted much influence and won the respect of his associates.

When Illinois became a state in 1818, Bond was elected its governor. His contemporary John Reynolds said of him:

Vandalia: Wilderness Capital of Lincoln's Land

> The honest and sincere friendship of the people for him made
> him the first governor of Illinois without opposition. The duties
> of this office were important, onerous, and difficult to perform.
> The change of laws, policy, and all, from a territorial government
> to a state government, required prudence, circumspection, and
> much wisdom. He possessed these qualifications and performed
> his duties to the general satisfaction of the people.[1]

In December, 1820, Shadrach Bond to perform his duties as
governor was in Vandalia where the General Assembly met for the
first time in the new capitol, a two-story frame building at the northwest corner of Johnson and Fifth Streets. The governor, according to
the constitution, was obliged to reside at the seat of government during
his four-year term of office. He lived at the home of his brother's
daughter Isabella Bond McLaughlin and her husband, Robert. The
governor's home was an unpretentious two-story frame with classic
arrangement of door and windows on the facade. Joseph C. Burtschi,
local historian, describes the only residence of which any one is
certain that served as a governor's mansion in Vandalia: "The building, large, very plain, painted white, stood along the lot line against
the sidewalk with no front yard. A garden and orchard were in the
rear." He remembers seeing the house when he was a boy.

Many distinguished guests were entertained in the governor's
mansion. Bond's hospitality and generosity became well-known. John
Reynolds describes Bond, the courteous host, and the gayety that prevailed where he entertained:

> He possessed a jovial and convivial spirit, and with his
> friends he enjoyed much happiness. These convivial parties were
> not based on gluttonness and intemperance; but they were sus-
> tained by the noble and generous hearts of the highest order of
> warm and congenial spirits. Bond possessed warm and ardent
> feelings and when excited in the society of his friends around
> the festive board, he not only was happy himself, but made all
> around him happy also. In these parties, he was the fountain of
> hilarity and good feelings and imparted it to all others around
> him.[2]

The term *capital gayety* has been used by Vandalia residents for generations. Indeed Bond gained such wide popularity as a host and
guest in society that it is very likely that the term originated when the
genial governor gave his lively parties.

But naturally Bond was not primarily concerned with the gayety
at the capital. He performed his duties ably, but not always did he and

14

the General Assembly meet with the measure of success that they had hoped. At this time the legislators were engrossed in the incorporation of a state bank. The measure, establishing a state bank with four branches, passed, but the state was the loser. Instead of helping business the legislative act caused more difficulties. The result was that the state lost hundreds of thousands of dollars. Governor Bond encouraged the improvement of the seat of government; a capital ought to have buildings worthy of its dignity. The first capitol was very plain and primitive. Buildings of almost a temporary nature—frame and log—surrounded the square. The first brick building was erected on the south side of the square in 1821 to house the capital's first bank.

Bond firmly recommended building institutions of learning and advocated strongly the importance of education. Notwithstanding the fact that the governors wanted public education, it appears in John Reynolds' description of Bond that college-trained men who appeared on the capital scene may have evoked some jealousy on the part of the self-educated men:

> He was not a lady-parlor scholar, who read the novels of lovesick swains and fainting girls; nor did he ever wash his face with cologne-water; but he was nature's nobleman, educated in the wide world of the human family, and his conscience and his sound judgment were his unerring preceptors. Some think a man is not intelligent or learned if he were not cudgelled thro a college or read "Robinson Crusoe" or the novel of "Goody Two Shoes."[3]

Although Reynolds wrote with zest concerning personalities whom he liked, one finds from other sources that Governor Bond easily established himself in public favor. His genial manner won him friends wherever he went. In his service to the state he must have acted with good judgment and intelligence. He conducted himself with resoluteness and honor. His diligent performance of his duties won for him esteem as the first governor of Illinois.

The following counties were formed in 1821: Lawrence, Greene, Sangamon, Pike, Hamilton, Montgomery, and Fayette. It is interesting to note that Pike County was extensive in size but sparse in population and within its boundaries was a small village situated on Lake Michigan. The settlement containing about a dozen houses and about seventy inhabitants was sixteen years later to receive its charter and to bear the Indian name *Chicago*. Fayette County, named for the famous French Marquis, was established on February 14, 1821.

Although Illinois was admitted as a free state, the first General Assembly in Kaskaskia whose members were in a large proportion natives of slave-holding communities enacted the "black laws," which later proved very severe to individuals who liberated their slaves. They were equally harsh to the runaway or to the liberated slaves without certificates of freedom. Toward the end of Governor Bond's term the excitement concerning slavery had not subsided in Illinois.

The officers whose labors and influence contributed so much to the progress of the infant commonwealth gave distinction to the Bond administration. The emergence of Illinois as a state meant that she must look to men who could be leaders to weld together the population under one government. The first lieutenant governor of the state was Pierre Ménard, an energetic, intellectual man who was quite active in the affairs of the Kaskaskia community. Since Ménard was born near Montreal, Canada, a provision was made in the constitution in order for him to qualify to hold office. He became a naturalized citizen only the year before his election. Ménard stood for the financial well-being of the state and protested vigorously against the state bank plan which failed.

Elias Kent Kane, a twenty-two-year-old New Yorker, served as the first secretary of state. Educated as a lawyer, he practiced for some time in Nashville, Tennessee. In 1815 he came to Kaskaskia. After the expiration of his term as secretary in 1822, he served in the state legislature, but after his election to the United States Senate in 1825, he went to Washington where he died in office ten years later. Kane is probably one of the most elusive figures that appeared on the capital scene. Theodore Pease calls him "the chief of the faction whenever he chose to exert his influence" and "the enigma of early Illinois politics." He asserts:

> Catalogs of his political activities, virtues, and vices can be found; again and again is seen his influence at work; but from all these can be drawn no picture of Kane himself. It is known that he was of a decayed aristocratic New York family, a graduate of Yale who came to Illinios to seek his fortune.[4]

Although John Thomas from St. Clair County became the first state treasurer, he served less than a year since his death occurred in

July, 1819. Robert K. McLaughlin served as the first treasurer in the new capital—a position which he held competently until 1823. Elijah Conway Berry served ably as auditor of public accounts from 1818-1831. Both Robert McLaughlin and Elijah Berry rest in the old State Burial Ground in Vandalia where many prominent early Illinoisans lie buried.

Shadrach Bond continued to be influential in the state after his governorship. During his administration he was strongly conservative on the subject of slavery, and after leaving office, he took an active part in the pro-slavery movement. In May, 1825, he was among those who participated at the reception of General Lafayette in Kaskaskia.

EDWARD COLES (1822-1826)

Governor Edward Coles headed in Illinois the early anti-slavery movement which won its first majority victory in the Northwest. He was born in Albemarle County, Virginia, in 1786. At Williamsburg Coles attended William and Mary College, which he left in 1807, a short time before the graduating examinations. A severe leg injury prevented him from taking his degree. One of his classmates there was John Tyler, who later became President of the United States. At the family mansion in Albemarle the young Edward early associated with such men as Patrick Henry, James Madison, and James Monroe—all of whom supported the theory on the rights of man.

In 1809 Coles found himself the owner of a certain number of slaves and a plantation which his father had bequeathed to him. During his college days the young Coles arduously studied the basic principles in Jefferson's Declaration of Independence "that all men are created equal" and found it impossible to reconcile himself to the fact that he lived in a state which held human beings in bondage. He determined to move from Virginia to a nonslave-holding state. However, an offer intervened which postponed his plans at that time. He accepted the appointment as private secretary to President James Madison in 1809. This position he held for six years during which time he enjoyed again the acquaintances and friendships of American statesmen in Washington.

Vandalia: Wilderness Capital of Lincoln's Land

It was in 1814 that Edward Coles opened a correspondence with Thomas Jefferson. Although both men resided in a slave-holding state, their views on the question of slavery were at variance with their neighbors. The remarkable letters of Coles to Jefferson and the celebrated answers of the author of the Declaration are well-worth reading. Coles appealed to Jefferson to devise a plan to liberate the slaves. Jefferson in his answer lamented the fact that the younger generation since the Revolution had not "sympathized with oppression wherever found, and proved their love of liberty beyond their own share of it." [5] He further said, "This enterprise is for the young, for those who can follow it up and bear it through to its consummation. It shall have all my prayers, and these are the only weapons of an old man." [6]

In his response Coles wrote:

> It was under these impressions that I looked to you, my dear Sir, as the first of our aged worthies to awaken our fellow-citizens from their infatuation to a proper sense of justice, and to the true interest of their country; and by proposing a system for the gradual emancipation of our slaves, at once to form a rallying point for its friends, who enlightened by your wisdom and experience, and supported and encouraged by your sanction and patronage, might look forward to a propitious and happy result. [7]

Such shows the earnest conviction of Edward Coles in wishing to eradicate slavery so that every man would have an equal right with every other man.

In 1815 Coles resigned his position as secretary to the President. In the autumn of that year he made a trip to the Northwest Territory for the purpose of finding a suitable location to live and to purchase land. He still entertained in his mind the plan to settle on the frontier in order to liberate his inherited slaves. However, when a serious misunderstanding arose between the United States and Russia, President Madison strongly urged Coles to undertake the diplomatic mission to Russia. Knowing him to be an able and discreet person, he felt confident in Coles' ability. Having been sent to Russia in a diplomatic capacity, Coles was accepted in official circles throughout Europe. He was presented to Louis XVIII of France by Albert Gallatin, American minister at that time. During his three months' stay in France, Coles was much in the company of General Lafayette.

His next visit was to England. In London during the spring of 1817 he was introduced to Morris Birkbeck by John Q. Adams, American minister to England. Adams informed Coles that Birkbeck was considered a scientific, skillful agriculturist as well as a gentleman of literary taste. Birkbeck then invited Coles to his large estate in Surrey where he showed him his methods in agriculture. It was at this time that Birkbeck expressed his desire to make the United States his home and from what information he had acquired by reading, he was inclined to prefer Ohio. At this point Coles offered substantial reasons for settling in the prairie region of Illinois when he would come to America.

When Coles returned to the United States, he was still determined to settle in Illinois. Knowing he would discharge any duty in a creditable manner, James Monroe conferred upon him the appointment of the Registrar of the Land Office at Edwardsville, Illinois. Coles carried with him from James Monroe a letter of introduction to Ninian Edwards. The letter, dated in Washington on April 13, 1818, attested to the excellent qualities of Coles, particularly his "sound judgment, great industry and fidelity." In that same year Coles moved to Illinois from Virginia with his ten Negroes. He granted each one his freedom on board the Ohio River before landing in Illinois. Within four years Coles had won such respect and recognition for his diplomacy and understanding in handling matters of the land office that he became a candidate for governor of the state.

In December, 1822, when the legislature convened at Vandalia, Governor Coles delivered his inaugural address in which he directed the attention of the legislators to restore the currency of the state to a fixed standard. Relieving the state of its embarrassment and directing it toward a sound currency was a vital problem in the new governor's mind; however, he mentioned other improvements needed in the state. He recommended just provisions for the abrogation of slavery. Many influential men were determined to introduce slavery into the state by calling a convention to alter the constitution. It was quite evident from the inaugural address that the new governor was to provide the leadership for the anti-convention group. A letter from Wansborough, Illinois, reached the governor a few weeks later. Morris Birkbeck wrote of his inaugural speech: "I should write to you even were it only for the pleasure of telling you that your speech has made a favorable impression in this quarter, and is highly commended, both as to matter and composition." [8]

The Illinois *Intelligencer,* the leading newspaper in the capital, referred to the governor at his inauguration as "His Excellency." Coles made it quite clear to the editors in a courteous letter that such a title was disagreeable to him. The first sentence of the letter will probably illustrate the tone and substance of it: "Our State Constitution gives to the person exercising the functions of the Executive, the appellation of *Governor*—a title which is specific, intelligible, and republican, and amply sufficient to denote the dignity of the office." [9]

At the very onset of his term Coles was confronted with a very strong group favoring alteration of the constitution to make Illinois a slave-holding state. The question excited much interest in Vandalia as well as throughout the state. Meetings were held in the capital, and committees were appointed for the purpose of fighting Governor Coles on the issue. The discussions in the meetings became noisy. The convention men attacked their opponents with bitter enmity. Even in the legislature the lawmakers were interrupted and insulted (it is no doubt it was violent at times) when they spoke against the convention. It was no surprise to hear them hurling names at one another such as "blackguard" or "liar."

A host of leading men of the state was arrayed against Coles such as ex-Governor Bond, Elias Kent Kane, Alexander Pope Field, and John Reynolds. In view of this situation Coles decided to take a strong hand. Fortunately the new governor possessed the advantages of education and political knowledge to cope with the circumstances. He lost no opportunity to communicate with the intellectuals who supported his views on the question, namely, Morris Birkbeck, David Blackwell, Daniel P. Cook, and Thomas Lippencott. Coles and his group rested on the basis of principles derived from the English political thinker John Locke, the French philosopher Rousseau, and the American spokesman of all freedom-loving humanity Thomas Jefferson. The group stood firmly on these principles in the face of the opposition.

Governor Coles lost no time in gaining control of the Illinois *Intelligencer,* and under his ownership the newspaper rallied to his cause, exerting a great influence against a constitution that would authorize the introduction of slavery. After all, the first newspapers on the frontier were actually established to serve as political organs or to print government papers. Under the *nom de plume* of Jonathan Freeman, Birkbeck wrote a series of letters, pamphlets, and articles against the convention scheme. Birkbeck's fiery letters and articles appeared in the leading newspapers of the state. He impressed upon the people's minds "the infamy of the proceedings of the Slave faction at Vandalia" and the *"impolicy* of Slavery." The convention group was defeated in the election in August, 1824, so forceful were the arguments of Birkbeck and his followers. When David Blackwell resigned his office as secretary of state in the following autumn, the governor offered Birkbeck the position in which he served for three months with competence.

The most interesting governor's message is perhaps the "extra session" speech which Coles sent November 18, 1824, for the purpose of the General Assembly to investigate the presidential election returns. According to law the assembly met in the first week of December. Clarence Walworth Alvord praises the speech as "one of the ablest and most statesman-like documents ever transmitted by any Governor of the State. Admirable in temper and style, it is marked by wise and sagacious recommendations." [10]

The interest in education was ever paramount in capital days. The legislators were confirmed in the opinion that it would be wise for the state to assist in the support of schools, but their constituents restrained them, feeling there were more pressing matters. On the subject of education Governor Coles appealed:

> There is no subject claiming the attention of the Legislature of more vital importance to the welfare of the state, and its future greatness and respectability, than the provisions which should be made for the education of the rising and succeeding generations. Intelligence and virtue are the main pillars in the temple of liberty. A government founded on the sovereignty of the people, and resting on and controlled by them, cannot be respectable, or even long endure, unless they are enlightened. To preserve and hand down to a continuous line of generations that liberty which was obtained by the valor and virtue of our forefathers, we must make provision for the moral and intellectual improvement of those who are to follow us, and who are to inherit and have the inestimable boon of self-government.[11]

21

The signal event of Governor Coles' administration was General Lafayette's visit to Illinois. When the members of the legislature learned that Lafayette was making a tour of the United States, they extended him in December, 1824, an invitation to visit Illinois. Governor Coles included along with the invitation a personal letter. Lafayette, expressing joy in finding the governor of Illinois a personal friend, responded that he would meet the governor at some point of the river, Kaskaskia or Shawneetown. It is interesting to note that Lafayette wrote in the lower left hand corner "His Excellency, Governor Coles, Illinois." Upon receipt of the general's answer Coles asked his aid-de-camp, the son of Alexander Hamilton (his name was William Stephen Hamilton), to meet Lafayette in St. Louis for the purpose of waiting on him and to inform the governor what route from St. Louis the general would pursue. When Lafayette arrived in Kaskaskia, it was Coles who made the address of welcome at the reception. It was indeed a bright spot in the otherwise difficult days for the governor to have his friend for whom he had such an affectionate and esteemed regard to be entertained at a reception in Illinois.

Although Coles performed his duties in a creditable manner, his opponents continued to persecute him for his courageous leadership of the anti-convention group. Repercussions menaced his status as an Illinois politician. Nevertheless, Edward Coles asserted able statesmanship in every situation. He left a distinguished record. He gave excellent advice on the election of judges, noteworthy ideas on the pardoning power of the governor, recommendations in regard to the Illinois and Michigan Canal, and he continually advocated the importance of education. He stood up well to the pressure groups whose prejudices against Negroes caused him incomparable pain and discomfort. Edward Coles' eminent record of public service to the state makes him an American of distinction. Certainly he expended his labor and directive efforts to further the practice of democracy in the United States.

NINIAN EDWARDS (1826-1830)

The third governor, Ninian Edwards (1775-1833), was the leader of an old faction that was soon to disappear in the frontier state. When the Edwards and anti-Edwards factions disintegrated, the Democratic and Whig parties emerged. Edwards was born in Montgomery County, Maryland, where private tutors instructed him. He attended Dickinson College in Pennsylvania, and after leaving, he began the study of law. He moved to Kentucky, practiced law, and became a member of the state legislature. He also served as chief justice.

In 1809 President Madison appointed Ninian Edwards governor of the Illinois Territory when it was constituted by an act of Congress. The seat of government was established at Kaskaskia on the banks of the Mississippi River. He held the post of territorial governor until 1818, and during that time he was active in handling Indian affairs on the frontier. In 1819 he became a United States Senator, serving competently, but resigned in 1824 when he accepted an appointment as minister of Mexico. An unfortunate situation occurred in which Edwards had made against the secretary of treasury some charges which he could not substantiate. It was necessary for Edwards to resign from his post as minister to Mexico. It seems that Edwards acted rashly on various occasions, and sound judgment was not one of his qualities.

Edwards turned to state politics, ran as a candidate for governor, and in his campaign arraigned the mismanagement of state finances, attacking vigorously the legislature. During his four-year term as governor, his early political prestige was waning. In Vandalia he did not seem to achieve the political success which was his in the past. However, from a cultural viewpoint the administration of Governor Edwards was quite successful. Movements to establish schools, the organization of a state historical society, and the beginning of literary activity were noteworthy intellectual efforts. Vandalia sprang up in 1819 offering at the onset a chance for the growth of intellectual life. The capital attracted lawyers, printers, surveyors, physicians, itinerant ministers, and men and women who represented traditions of culture and education. It was not at all surprising that in such a short period of time the little frontier town was the center of culture.

Several colleges sprang into being in the state. The pioneer was beginning to learn the need of education and religion. At first he pushed them aside as unessential. He opposed taxes save for necessities; schools and learning seemed out of accord with frontier needs.

He definitely opposed religion as superstitious and hypocritical. However, the Baptists with their zealous John Mason Peck, the Methodists with their forceful Peter Cartwright, and the Presbyterians with their educated clergy eagerly pursued missionary activity in the Midwestern area. Indeed they rendered a public service to the frontiersmen by helping to establish schools. There was need of college-trained ministers. Since the first colleges were denominational, the Illinois Legislature did not give permission to grant degrees for sometime. The school act of 1827 provided no taxation without the consent of the person taxed for school purposes. Of course there were private schools available, but as one would conclude they were open only to those who could pay. John Mason Peck built between O'Fallon and Lebanon the Rock Spring Theological Seminary and High School, the beginning which developed into Shurtleff College, which is located near Alton. In the town of Lebanon, McKendree College, established by the Methodists, sprang into being. A group of Yale men were building "a greater Yale on the Illinois Prairies" in Jacksonville; the institution of learning was called Illinois College. Knox College was founded in 1837 at Galesburg under the original name Prairie College during Governor Duncan's administration.

Like John Reynolds, Ninian Edwards lived in Belleville, an old Illinois town, located south of St. Louis. His residence, however, disappeared, but Governor Reynolds' home, built in 1820, survives. Ninian Edwards is not to be confused with his son Ninian Wirt Edwards, who married a sister of Abraham Lincoln's wife. Ninian Edwards not only served as both territorial and state governor, but he represented Illinois as its first United States Senator. Jesse B. Thomas, president of the convention that adopted the first Illinois Constitution in 1818, and Ninian Edwards were chosen by the state legislature to be the first United States Senators from Illinois.

JOHN REYNOLDS (1830-1834)

The fourth governor of Illinois was the frontiersman John Reynolds (1788-1865). He was born in Montgomery County, Pennsylvania, reared near Knoxville, Tennessee, and at the age of twelve settled in Kaskaskia, Illinois. He saw military service in the War of

1812. After he had set up a law practice in Cohokia in 1814, he rose steadily in politics. From 1818-1825 he served as an associate justice in the Illinois Supreme Court. In 1826 and in 1828 he was a member of the General Assembly. John Reynolds favored slavery and ran rough-shod over those who opposed him on the issue. He did not distinguish himself in the legal profession, but he succeeded well as a politician. He was wise enough to conceal his "book learnin'" among the poor folk when he was campaigning. His "book larnin'," however, never attained the degree of scholarly knowledge, although Reynolds himself might have felt he was a scholar.

Nevertheless, Illinoisans are indebted to Reynolds for his two books *The Pioneer History of Illniois* (1852) and *My Own Times* (1855). Perhaps a brief explanation of the first book will serve to record Reynolds' efforts in the field of writing. The volume which covers the years 1673-1818 contains information that is valuable to authorities in the field of history although it is not always reliable. It is quite evident that Governor Reynolds is inclined to eulogize pioneers whom he found admirable. His work has the authority of personal observation but not of scholarship. Furthermore, his lack of literary craftsmanship is manifest, for the narrow range of his education is apparent in his style which lacks force, directness, and often clarity. However, it is gratifying that he attempted such a labor which must have had its degree of exhaustion. When reading Reynolds' book, one does not feel he is witnessing a picturesque history, but he is aware that the actors in the drama are significant and well worth knowing.

In the introduction of *The Pioneer History of Illinois* he states:

> Time is rapidly sweeping off from the scene of action the pioneers of our country; and even the recollection of their actions will soon be forgotten, if no attempt is made to perpetuate the history of this worthy and noble race of men.

The signal event during Reynolds' governorship was the Black Hawk War in 1832. Black Hawk, the leader of the Sauk and Fox, crossed the Mississippi River to plant corn along the Rock River in northern Illinois, claiming that an injustice had been done to the Indians to push them out of the state. The Sauk and Foxes began to terrorize the white settlers by their night raids. Cabins were burned and people were killed. When Governor Reynolds called for volunteers from the state militia, many answered his appeal. Young politicians marched with the volunteers mustered from all over the state. It was the circular issued by Governor Reynolds that brought the citizen-soldiers into action:

> Your country requires your services. The Indians have assumed a hostile attitude, and have invaded the State in violation of the treaty of last summer .The British band of Sacs and other hostile Indians, headed by Black Hawk, are in possession of the Rock River country, to the great terror of the frontier inhabitants.

The remaining part of the circular exhorts the people to offer their services to defend their country.

Some of the most prominent men of this area enlisted to protect the northwestern frontier of Illinois. Among them were Frederick Reaman (sometimes it is spelled Remann), Robert Blackwell, Elijah C. Berry, William L. D. Ewing, and Augustus Synder. The group from Fayette County marched to the mouth of Rock River where General Atkinson received the men into the service of the United States and took command. Reynolds, styled both the "Old Ranger" and the "war governor," remained with the force. President Jackson recognized Reynolds as Major-General. It seems that the governor's presence in the army promoted concord among the regular troops and volunteers. When Reynolds heard of Major Stillman's defeat, he wrote an order by candlelight on that evening calling for more volunteers and dispatched it the next morning to all the counties. It was not until September, 1832, that a treaty was made with the Sac and Fox tribes making the northwestern part of Illinois safe for development by white settlers.

Although he acted well his part in the Indian skirmishes, Illinoisans cannot forget the shameful conduct of John Reynolds toward Edward Coles when he acted as the presiding judge of the Circuit Court at Edwardsville in 1824. The pro-slavery men had instituted a suit against Coles for setting at liberty ten Negro slaves without giving bond. Judge Reynolds decided several points of law against Coles in direct opposition to the opinion of several of the best lawyers in the state. The jury found a verdict of $2,000 against Coles. However, in January, 1825, the legislature passed an act releasing all penalties incurred under the act of 1819 (including those sued for) under which

Coles was prosecuted. Reynolds' involvement caused a blot upon his character that persisted through the years. It seems appropriate in these pages to mention Reynolds' implication although the suit is examined in a later chapter.

Theodore Pease has in epigrammatic fashion painted a word portrait of John Reynolds in his book *The Story of Illinois:*

> John Reynolds, in later years the historian of pioneer Illinois in volumes that are literary curiosities, had a smattering of education which he strove to stretch to the appearance of erudition. Always an office-seeker, always searching for the popular side of every issue, fawning on his friends when he needed them and discarding them when they could no longer serve him, he shuffled his way through Illinois politics from 1818 to the days of the Civil War. That such a man could become governor and congressman is proof that the day of aristocratic dignity in Illinois politics has passed.[12]

Although such is one astute chronicler's view of the man, historians have been uniformly unfavorable toward the governor. The Reynolds personality, however, made itself felt among the masses. He spoke plainly using humorous illustrations and charmed them in his masterful electioneering. In his book *My Own Times* Reynolds reveals party excitement, his success with "stump speeches," party rancor, and trickery that existed during the gubernatorial election of 1830. Such material secured at first-hand is valuable to later historians. The distinction of having held positions in all branches of the government—executive, judicial, and legislative—makes Reynolds a political figure of unusual interest to Illinoisans.

WILLIAM LEE DAVIDSON EWING (1834)

Upon the election of John Reynolds to Congress in 1834, he resigned as governor November 17, and since Governor-elect Duncan's term did not begin until December 3, the lieutenant governor W. L. D. Ewing (1795-1846) served the intervening days as chief executive. Ewing's prominence as a citizen was recognized when he was appointed among others as a trustee to the town of Vandalia in 1821. Five years later he was elected clerk of the House of Representatives. In 1828 he was receiver of the Vandalia Land District; his reports in this position indicate he was a man of considerable education. In 1830 he was elected representative and made speaker of the House. He then advanced to the State Senate. His letters written from the United States Senate further indicate his adequate education and competence.

Ewing responded to Governor Reynolds' appeal in the Black Hawk War "to protect the frontier and preserve the honor of the state." In 1832 he served for a period of time in espionage to ascertain location of Indians. It was with distinction that he served his state in this war. Upon his election to the United States Senate in 1835, he went to Washington for a period of two years and then returned to Vandalia to take active part again in state legislation.

It was General Ewing who so vigorously opposed the Whigs of Sangamon when they maneuvered to move the capital to Springfield. An extra session after the bill had passed was called in the summer of 1837. Ewing at this session charged in no subdued manner the Springfield delegation with "chicanery and trickery." He protested that Lincoln and his colleagues had sold out to the internal improvement faction, in promising support to every measure in order to gain votes for the bill to remove the capital to Springfield. Lincoln answered the challenge by a speech that accomplished his purpose. It has been a part of Vandalia tradition that friends intervened to prevent a duel between the high-spirited Ewing and the bitter Lincoln.

In 1838 General Ewing was elected to the House of Representatives. Lincoln was nominated by the Whigs for speaker but was defeated on the fourth ballot by Ewing. The Sangamon delegation and many other members did not adopt Ewing's viewpoint on retention of the capital in Vandalia. Attempts to amend the appropriation bill were futile. Springfield had donated $50,000 to pay the cost of a new statehouse. The state would match the amount. Unyielding forces compelled Ewing to abandon his attempt to keep the capital at Vandalia.

At Ewing's death in 1846 he held the office of auditor in the statehouse at Springfield. Vandalia residents remembered him as a gentleman of fine principles and of forceful character. They considered him a zealous statesman who exerted influence and for a brief term presided over the destinies of the young republic of Illinois. Always a popular figure in Vandalia, General Ewing was regarded as a man of ability and generosity, and especially the fifth governor of Illinois was widely known in the state as a powerful opponent of Abraham Lincoln.

JOSEPH DUNCAN (1834-1838)

Joseph Duncan was born February 22, 1794, in Paris, Kentucky. His father Joseph Duncan was a major in the United States Army. His son, however, received very little schooling but showed a keen interest when he became a lawmaker in offering the advantages of education to Illinoisans. The young Joseph served in the frontier campaigns of the War of 1812. He was elected to the Senate from Jackson County in 1824. At this time he supported a bill for a public educational system. The bill which Duncan introduced relating to free schools was passed in 1825. Unfortunately, it was repealed four years later. In 1826 Duncan defeated Daniel Cook, who was running for a fourth successive term in Congress. Duncan remained at Washington until his election as governor of Illinois in 1834.

When Duncan became the chief executive of the state, he continued to advocate the need of a free school system. Furthermore, he continued to support the internal improvements plan which involved more than ten million dollars for roads, rivers, and railroads. Governor Duncan along with Stephen Douglas and Orville Hickman Browning refused to support the scheme espoused by Abraham Lincoln. Although they supported the idea of internal improvements, they did not recommend the legislative act that passed. Likewise, Duncan did not give his stamp of approval to the act which almost wrecked financially the state.

It is well known that Lincoln and the Sangamon County delegation traded their votes on the improvement system for the location of the next capital in their county at Springfield. Vandalia was established to remain the capital for twenty years; the residents hoped if they erected a suitable building the legislators would consider Vandalia, and there would be no relocation of the capital. The legislative bill, nevertheless, removing the capital to Springfield was passed through the vigorous efforts and political intrigue (some legislators referred to the maneuvering in stronger language) of the Sangamon group which included Lincoln.

But the legislators were not too busy to perform Christian duties. The members of the House of Representatives attended the funeral of Benjamin A. Clark of Wayne County on Sunday, January 10, 1836. He had died Saturday evening. His body was interred in the one-half acre set aside for legislators and officers in the State Burial Ground. On Monday, January 11, the members voted to give their day's pay to the widow and infant children of the thirty-six-year-old legislator.

Joseph Duncan and other men of limited education and natural ability pursued the idea of organizing a system of public education. Likewise, the well-educated men used their talent to urge thinking on the matter. James Hall in his magazine had made Illinoisans aware of their illiterate population and the necessity of enlightenment in a democracy. John Mason Peck was informing his readers in *A Guide for Emigrants* that many adults were unable to read and write. In *A Gazetteer of Illinois* he urged, "A complete common school education must be organized." Thousands of children in Illinois were attending no school at all. The legislators were applying their efforts to a realization of a public education for all. A state Education Convention was held in Vandalia, December 5, 1834. The young legislator from Sangamon Abraham Lincoln was elected as a delegate to this convention. Intelligent interest in education persisted throughout Duncan's regime. Three years later one finds an appeal for the establishment of the office of superintendent of public instruction.

On December 9, 1836, Alexander Pope Field, Secretary of State, directed by Governor Duncan, laid before the Senate a message in writing, a part of which dealt with the subject of education:

> In all ages and under every circumstance, education has decided the relative greatness of men and nations. Placed beyond its genial influence, man becomes a savage, and a nation, a wandering band of lawless depredators. Education under all forms of government, constitutes the first principle of human happiness; and especially, is it important in a country, where the sovereignty is vested in the people.[13]

He then refers to the bill he submitted in 1825 for the establishment of free schools.

Since then, I have reflected much on the subject, and am
more fully convinced, that such policy, is perfectly consistent
with the rights and interest of every citizen, and that it is the
only one calculated to sustain our democratic republican institutions; in fact, general education is the only means by which
the rich and the poor, can be placed upon the same level, and
by which, intelligence and virtue, can be made to assume its
proper elevation, over ignorance and vice.[14]

Certainly Governor Duncan conveyed the impression of a
purposeful behavior towards the welfare of the state. His position
was basically sound on the questions that were to be solved. When
incidents seem to appear other than what they actually were, Duncan
often discerned the truth. For example, in November, 1837, occurred
the assassination of Elijah Parish Lovejoy, who expressed too
freely his opinions of mob law in his newspaper *The Observer*.
Leaders like John Mason Peck, however, denied that Lovejoy was
such a martyr of freedom. They actually looked upon him as a dangerous agitator. Lovejoy's advocation of hanging leaders of pro-slavery
mobs was not met with Duncan's approval.

THE STATEHOUSE

The most appealing relic of Joseph Duncan is the old Statehouse
in which he served. He was the first governor to occupy the imposing
old structure that still graces the original plot of ground surveyed for

the Illinois capitol. One receives a certain impression of kinship to Duncan when he reads the message to the Senate in December, 1836, concerning this memorable building:

> In consequence of the dilapidated and falling condition of the old State House, the public officers, mechanics, and citizens of this place, believing that the legislature would have no place to convene or hold their session, have built the House you now occupy. This work has been done in a time, and under circumstances which evinces an industry, zeal and public spirit that does honor to the place and commands our grateful acknowledgments, and I hope their services and expenses will be promptly remunerated.[15]

Duncan served the longest period of time of any governor in the Statehouse. He was the first governor under whose administration the young Lincoln served as representative. In the spacious entrance hall one sees a land grant signed by Joseph Duncan, the only known tribute to his memory in the old Statehouse. One can say much in praise of Duncan's governorship, but he is chiefly remembered for his interest in education. He has left his imprint upon Illinois history as an arduous advocate for the system of public education which has flourished so well in the state.

THOMAS CARLIN (1838-1839)

Thomas Carlin, the last governor while Vandalia served as the state capital, was inaugurated December 7, 1838. Thomas Carlin, the Democrat, had defeated Cyrus Edwards, the Whig. The oath of office was administered to him in the Hall of the House of Representatives. The Senate repaired to the House and the governor delivered verbally his address in which he stressed the cause of education: "The most effectual means for advancing the interests of the people, and developing the resources of a country, is the general diffusion of knowledge."

Thomas Carlin seems to be the most elusive figure in the pages of Vandalia's history. Even though he was elected governor, nothing seems to signify that he was the leading man of his party. Harry Pratt gives a certain portrait of Vandalia's last governor in the introduction of his book *Lincoln, 1809-1839:* "Thomas Carlin, the incoming Governor was a tall, spare man, with a pale face partially offset by his red hair and beard. His generally feeble appearance was augmented by weak eyes. His address was a contrast with Duncan's being full of hope and cheer for the Democrats and full of words of praise for Van Buren."

The new governor also urged the internal improvements program, and the legislature continued the policy. Fortunately, Carlin began to see as Douglas, Browning, and Duncan that the policy of such a system was ruinous, and seeing its failure, he experienced a change of thought on the subject. However, like Duncan, he could not prevent its passing the assembly. The costly legislative folly which found its birth in the minds of dreamers like Lincoln was in evidence throughout the state where excavations remained incompleted. In July, 1839, the capital was removed to Springfield, and thus ended the lofty position to which Vandalia was elevated at her inception.

SEVEN GOVERNORS
1. John Reynolds, **Pioneer History of Illinois** (Chicago, 1887), p. 327
2. Ibid., p. 324
3. Ibid., pp. 323-324
4. T. C. Pease, **The Frontier State** (Springfield, 1918), p. 94
5. C. A. Alvord, **Governor Edward Coles** (Springfield, 1920), p. 25
6. Ibid., p. 26
7. Ibid., p. 29
8. Ibid., p. 54
9. Ibid., p. 55
10. Ibid., p. 186
11. Ibid., pp. 274-275
12. T. C. Pease, **The Story of Illinois** (Chicago, 1949), p. 108
13. Scrapbook of Joseph Duncan (Illinois State Historical Survey, Urbana) p. 198
14. Ibid., p. 198
15. Ibid., p. 198

ORIGINAL BUILDINGS
AND PLACES

Vandalia has had only one famous period in history—the time it served as the state capital of Illinois when it was a wilderness settlement. The history of the town in terms of the Midwest is long; few of its buildings, however, are of any notable age. Vandalia will be disappointing if one hastily scans its profusion of late nineteenth and twentieth century buildings. It appears upon casual glance that the frontier atmosphere has been replaced by modernity unless one follows the route of high points traced by the historian. For history survives in the great old Statehouse, the property formerly owned by the capital artist James W. Berry on which the Little Brick House stands, the old State Burial Ground, the Evans Library, the Blackwell Printery, the Evans Log Cabin, A. P. Field Dwelling, the Vandalia Hotel, and the Presbyterian Church which houses the Daniel Boone of church bells. They remain as monuments of the early commonwealth which existed in a small village in the heart of a forest. But much of the forest timber has been cut down, and the land lies stripped of almost all its ancient monarchs; however, other trees have grown in their stead and have attained a size to be honored as memorials to the ancient giants of capital days.

There are no crumbling abbeys or castles of past ages, but only simple structures stand as phantoms of departed glory when everything was pointing to the future instead of the past. These primitive buildings stand as rather melancholy and uninteresting unless one is familiar enough with their part in the baby footsteps of a great state. The traveler to Vandalia will possess a greater appreciation if his mind is filled with historical associations connected with the places by reading about them before his visit.

The industrial hosts have advanced menacingly toward the buildings which existed during capital days. The architecture of the period has almost been lost through both demolition and remodeling. The frontier capitol architecturally is the most impressive structure. The Vandalia Hotel and the Blackwell Printery are survivors that have held on with remarkable vitality, despite undergoing many changes of appearance. The log cabin which still stands represents well the type of home in which the early settlers lived and adjusted themselves to a primitive environment. One dwelling is worthy of mention, although it was not erected during capital days, by the very fact that it resembles the early homes as evidenced by authentic drawings. That place is now called the Little Brick House. Its early history is undetermined, but classic arrangement of door and windows in the modified Georgian style resembles the homes of the early period. It is idle for any Vandalian to protest progress and lament the loss of historic buildings. Alas, such a change is the law of growth!

EVANS LOG CABIN

THE EVANS LOG CABIN

Early settlers used almost universally the log cabin for their dwelling. These habitations in the clearings were not those of unlettered people as some believe. A goodly proportion of literate people settled Vandalia. Many families who lived in log cabins were well clothed and well fed. One seems to be impressed with the fact that Lincoln began his life in a log cabin. It means to some that he rose from dire poverty. It seems improbable that one would think in this manner when he realized that many such cabins as the Evans dwelling dotted the countryside of the Midwest in the 'twenties and 'thirties.

The log cabin has almost disappeared from the national scene. One often sees these dwellings reconstructed but rarely views an original one that gives an authentic glimpse into frontier living. The log cabin was built in 1831 by Akin Evans and has been carefully preserved by his grandson Charles Akin Evans to remind the present and future generations of how early settlers lived. It is a reminder, too, although the idea is unrealistic, that the log cabin delineates for an American a symbol of equal opportunity for all. Since Lincoln was born in one, Americans see in it the ideal of democracy and belief that any man may rise by his native abilities and occupy the White House. It was the vote-conscious politician who first focused attention on the log cabin as a humble, simple shelter. Nowhere is the belief that illustrious men came from log cabins better symbolized than in Lincoln. The cabin was three years old when Lincoln came to Vandalia. Likewise, it stands as a symbol associated with the great statesman as well as a reminder of how the pioneers lived.

The land grant (9½ x 15 inches in size) from the United States of America to Akin Evans is still in existence. The seal of the General Land Office, affixed at the lower left-hand corner, is unreadable, but Andrew Jackson's signature, which appears on the certificate, is still very clear. The grant contains the description of the tract containing eighty acres. Akin Evans purchased the land March 7, 1831, "in the Year of our Lord, One thousand, eight hundred and thirty one and of the Independence of the United States the Fifty fifth." It seems incredible that shortly after its purchase the taxes on the eighty acres was the total sum of eighty cents. On the site where the log cabin was built another farmhouse stands three miles south of Vandalia on the Carlyle Road. In 1962 the grandson sold the farm that had been in the Evans family 131 years.

In the early 1930's Charles Evans moved the log cabin to a picturesque spot, located about four miles east of Vandalia on the Cumberland Road. The log cabin consists of two rooms downstairs— a combination living room and bedchamber and a small kitchen at the rear in the form of a lean-to. A fireplace is a part of the larger room. The upstairs bedroom is entered by way of an outside stairway. Akin Evans' service as sheriff and state senator during capital days attests to the fact that he was not an unlettered man. His penmanship as well as his expression of thoughts found in journals and papers indicate his literacy. Indeed it is misleading to equate the builder and owner of this rare bit of Americana with illiteracy. Akin was buried in 1861 in the Evans Cemetery, established during capital days on the original tract bought from the United States. His father Jeremiah was buried there in 1836.

In making a visit to the cabin, one can relive by imagination pioneer days. He can almost hear the howl of the wolf or the hum of the spinning wheel. The dwelling was under construction at the same time that Lincoln was floating a canoe down the Sangamon River that was to take him to New Salem. The year before, Abe had helped his father build a cabin on Goose Nest Prairie. So the Evans cabin, cut out of the prairie timber, reminds one of the families who came to live on Illinois soil. It has seen many winters, lean times with hunger and cold and good times with plenty and warmth. Today on the scenic knoll overlooking the old Cumberland Road, it survives in quiet importance.

THE ALEXANDER POPE FIELD DWELLING

Surviving from early capital days, the Field dwelling is Vandalia's famous home, the scene of brilliant gatherings. It occupies the northwest corner of Fourth and Johnson Streets, the location of which is only one block south of the Statehouse. The two-story frame house with a simple architectural design—the classic arrangement of door and windows—was built in 1834 on its present location. The entrance door at the left and two windows on the first floor and three on the second were arranged proportionately in Georgian style. Judging from photographs, one might say the residence resembled the Mark Twain House in Hannibal, although it was not built flush with the sidewalk. A white picket fence originally enclosed the property.

Unfortunately, the Field residence did not escape the bad taste of later additions that mar some of Vandalia's original buildings. Had it not been remodeled this dwelling would have possessed value in exemplifying the domestic style of architecture during capital days. In the early part of the 1900's the house was extensively enlarged, and the building spree did nothing for its architectural design. The so-called improvements corrupted its trim pattern. But regardless of its distasteful appearance, it was the home of the secretary of state who entertained like a prince. Among his guests were prominent legislators, senators, governors, and state officers. It is no doubt that Lincoln, Douglas, Baker, Cartwright, and other figures who dominated capital society ate and drank here amid sprightly conversation with their gracious host whom people addressed "Colonel Field." This tall, handsome man who towered six foot, two inches, deeply impressed people with his convivial habits, polished manners, and his ability to converse well.

In early Illinois history Colonel Field was a prominent figure who by his ability, power, and influence was excelled by few other statesmen. He was born in Louisville, Kentucky, November 30, 1800. The Pope name had been made illustrious by his uncles Judge Nathaniel Pope and Governor John Pope of Arkansas. Field attended Transylvania University in Kentucky. In 1818 he went to Kaskaskia with Judge Pope but settled at Jonesboro, located in Union County. Four years later he became a candidate for office to the Illinois Legislature. He was elected to the House of Representatives to the Third General Assembly which met in December, 1822.

At a pro-slavery meeting in February, 1823, Field was appointed on a committee to draft resolutions and an address to be presented to the people in justification of repealing the constitution of 1818. A meeting was held again in February at which the resolutions and address were reported. With Field's intense interest in this matter and his efforts to secure a convention, he became a leader of the pro-slavery forces. He continued to serve in the House of Representatives in the Fifth and Sixth General Assemblies.

Governor Edwards in 1828 appointed Field secretary of state, which position he held during the remaining time that Vandalia was the capital. However, Field absented himself from the capital at such long intervals that Governor Edwards found it necessary to rebuke him. Field was practicing law in Jonesboro instead of performing his duties in Vandalia. The governor made it clear to Field that his continuance as secretary depended upon his future attention to the office. During his service from 1828-1840 Field was considered an able statesman; furthermore, his law practice continued to be successful. His speeches were impressive, his arguments forceful, and the press praised his efforts. Undoubtedly Field possessed a vigorous intellect as well as a magnetic personality.

A strong friendship existed between John Reynolds and Field. Their feelings for each other had been quite genial for many years if one judges from their correspondence. In a letter of September, 1829, Reynolds writes:

> It is useless for me to say anything to you in relation to my friendship and feelings toward you. You have no friends who can be elected governor that will do more for you than I will. You have the evidence of that many years past.[1]

The excerpt in some degree attests to Field's influence on others. Reynolds in turn used his influence to help Field when he requested assistance. According to correspondence Field made a claim upon the United States Government for services rendered as an *aid-de-camp* during the Black Hawk War. The correspondence between him and Reynolds, however, indicates that he did not receive the money for his services although Reynolds presumbably exerted some effort. In 1840 when he was in Washington, Reynolds called upon the Secretary of War to urge an allowance for Field's services, but Reynolds informed Field that it was doubtful that he would obtain the money.

A letter from his daughter Eleanor, who was a student at Ménard Academy, brings one very close to the secretary. The letter is not post-marked but across the upper right hand corner is written *Prairie du Rocher.* The simple address on the communication (there is no envelope) is:

Col. A. P. Field
Vandalia
Illinois

The following is the letter:

Ménard Academy
Kaskaskia, June 12th
1839

Dearest Father,
It is with the greatest pleasure I now address one so dear to me. I have written twice to Mother, but not received one letter

39

from her. I think very hard of it indeed perhaps she has written: —but I have not received any letters. I have to study very hard as we are to be examined in two or three days. We have got four new scholars from Springfield and expect several [*sic*] more soon. and one from town. As I have written so often, I have not any news to tell you. I have not heard a word from Vandalia since I left, nor has Miss Malinda Berry. I should like to know when you are coming to see me. I should like to see you and Mother very much: you said you were coming down in September. I hope you have not given it up.

Give my love to Mother and all my friends. I hope you will write to me soon. I remain your affectionate and devoted Child, Eleanor Field.[2]

Although Colonel Field served as secretary when the state was democratic, he was an influential Whig; however, he lost his office because of his political affiliations after Vandalia was no longer the capital. In 1841 General Harrison appointed him Secretary of Wisconsin Territory. At the breaking out of the War Between the States, Field was living in New Orleans where he suffered many threats and abuses for his loyalty to the Federal Government.

The old dwelling was sold to Daniel Gregory whose heirs retained it until the last few years. Alexander Pope Field is well remembered in Vandalia as a secretary of state who was prominent in the political and social affairs of the capital and as a criminal lawyer who handled his cases with such intellectual vigor and logic that he was highly successful. Many pioneers of Vandalia had a warm spot in their hearts for this gifted man of striking appearance whom they affectionately called "Alec Field." And his home remains in their memory as one of the social centers in the capital.

THE VANDALIA HOTEL

The Vandalia Hotel, commonly called the Flack House, is the only inn still standing today that dispensed its hospitality to the lawmakers of the General Assembly. The frame, two and a half story building was removed from its original Gallatin Street site to the south side of Johnson Street between Fourth and Fifth. Its original appearance, however, has been changed somewhat. It is no architectural gem since its remodeling, but fortunately it did not suffer such corruption as did the Field residence. Almost all the buildings in the newly established capital were simple but substantial shelters. Timber was abundant in this area; likewise, the buildings were either log cabins or frame houses with the exception of some public buildings which were of brick construction.

THE VANDALIA HOTEL (FLACK HOUSE)

The Vandalia Hotel was built in the early 1830's by George Leidig, a member of the Ernst Colony. He advertised in the newspapers that he could accommodate one hundred legislators with sufficient stable room for the horses belonging to the guests. A few years later Abner Flack operated the hotel. One will find that the hotels and taverns charged comparatively the same prices. A night's lodging cost only 12½¢ while it cost 50¢ to stable the horses for the night. However, the horse's feed cost only 18 3/4¢ while the guest's breakfast or supper amounted to the sum of 25¢; the guest's dinner cost him 37½¢. Peach or apple brandy, gin, and cordial could be purchased at 25¢ for a half pint. [3] James Hall's tabulation of food prices in the *Illinois Monthly Magazine* also supports the fact that relatively low costs prevailed.

The writer of this book was present at the time George Whiteman, grandson of George Leidig, showed Joseph Burtschi a menu used in

41

the Vandalia Hotel during the 1830's. The menu was one of the few items that survived the fire at the Leidig residence where the records of the Vandalia Hotel were consumed in the flames. The guests at the inn must have eaten with zest the grouse, a prairie fowl, found in abundance on the open areas. In the words of James Hall "the flesh is delicate and finely flavored." Wild turkey was not reserved for festive occasions; it was a frequent viand on the table since the innkeeper was able to purchase the fowls for the paltry sum of 12½¢ a piece. The inn prided itself in serving fine food and choice liqior.

The Vandalia Hotel played its role in the social activities of the capital. Social life on the frontier did not come later to the capital; it did not have to wait for a more thickly settled population. If there were stories of log-rolling, quilting bees, and house-warming, they were apparently relegated into the background. Barbecues and horse racing were occasions of fun in Vandalia. There was rude and boisterous activity in the grog-shops or taverns where an abundance of whiskey and brandy was offered for sale. The public square was thronged with office seekers, and almost all the legislators were pressed by appeals from them to sample the liquids. Indeed the session days of the capital attracted large gatherings of people to the social mecca of Illinois. The arduous labors of pioneering did not affect the ladies and gentlemen who participated in the capital festivities.

Accordingly, the Vandalia Hotel was a gay place when the General Assembly was in session. In the candlelighted rooms of the inn state officers, lawmakers, men of influence, and their ladies attended parties, cotillions, and banquets. Unquestionably Lincoln frequented the inn, but only one incident is actually recorded of his presence. The youthful legislator attended a party in the hotel one evening. His shabby appearance and unbecoming manners according to feminine standards were major shortcomings that Vandalia belles could not easily overlook. Lincoln was aware that the local young ladies were avoiding him so he asked Matilda Flack, wife of Milton and a relative of the proprietor, to dance. During the frolic Lincoln stepped on her dress and tore it. His great concern at the mishap counterbalanced his awkwardness. He was so personable and

42

genuinely sorry about the unfortunate incident that Matilda Flack could not be disgruntled with the unhappy young man. [4]

But Stephen Douglas had no difficulty finding a dancing partner. In comparison to the charming and gifted young Douglas, Lincoln was dull and clumsy. Perhaps the young, feminine minds of Vandalia were placing too much emphasis on physical attributes and refined manners. But was it not this young legislator that was agitating the removal of the capital from Vandalia? He may not have been a compelling figure on the dance floor but in the Statehouse he was maneuvering smoothly to relocate the capital. He was making bargains and granting favors to the legislators always with an eye on the votes needed to locate the capital at Springfield where he had opened a law practice. Later when the good of the nation was at stake, it was the same carelessly dressed, awkward lawyer whose strength, intellect, and devotion to principle made him a compelling figure in the nation's capital.

The visitor views the old inn almost ruefully as he notes its modern appearance and the slight it suffers historically. One can become buried in his reflections of the glory it has known and become bewildered into what complacence Illinoisans have fallen to allow it so little recognition. But wise and silent, the venerable inn appears unmoved by its nameless grief.

THE OLD STATE BURIAL GROUND

Of the thousands of visitors who annually stream into Vandalia, many are interested in the old State Burial Ground that stands on a wooded knoll in the southeastern part of town. Primarily, it is a tribute to the vision and fortitude of the pioneers who settled this rugged area and to the politicians who appeared on the scene to legislate the laws of the state. This small plot of ground harbors the remains of Ferdinand Ernst, Robert and Isabella McLaughlin, James W. Berry, Colonel Greenup, Mary Harrison Posey Hall (wife of James Hall), Robert Blackwell, and many others who played a part in the activities of the infant state. The graves have marked headstones and obelisks, many of which are so worn by time and weather as to be unreadable.

43

Vandalia: Wilderness Capital of Lincoln's Land

The old State Burial Ground dates from 1823 when the Illinois Legislature passed an act conveying a piece of land to contain one and one-half acres for that purpose. Twelve years later the legislature passed an act to lay off a certain portion for burial of the legislators and governmental officers who might die at the time they were discharging their duties at the capital. Transportation difficulties were such that pioneers were forced to wait long periods of time to travel. As a result, it was necessary for the legislature to provide a burial ground for its members. The obelisk erected to the memory of five legislators who died during the sessions was moved to the South Hill Cemetery, the area where Vandalia residents are now buried. It is conjecture that the five bodies were also removed. Why the monument was removed from the old State Burial Ground has always been an enigma to present-day Vandalia residents.

Edwards Street, named for the third governor of Illinois, runs east and west on the north side of the burial ground while the entrance faces Second Street. As visitors from all over the United States and foreign lands enter the graveled pathway, they learn of obscure persons who lie buried in this historic spot and try to decipher the inscriptions on the tombstones. They inquire the fate of those whose "frail memorials" are succumbing to the elements. Most of the epitaphs acquaint the visitor with only the date of birth and of death. The inscriptions would have been more interesting if as Joseph Addison once said "elegance of expression and justness of thought" had characterized them. But no doubt there was little time even for men of learning to put into execution a thoughtful epitaph. If one conceives the idea of education from the turn of the inscriptions that reveal more than merely date of birth and death, one will realize that the early settlers did no dishonor to the dead. Especially such is true of the slab marking the grave of James Hall's wife. The epitaph reflects the author's sentiment:

She was very lovely, and greatly beloved.
Filial piety towards God
And benevolence to her fellow creatures
Marked her whole life;
And
The peace which passeth all understanding
Blessed her dying hour.

44

Original Buildings and Places

In 1823 when the act providing a burial ground was passed, this plot of ground no doubt contained the oldest native trees, namely, oak, walnut, hickory, ash, elm, wild black cherry, gum, dogwood, sassafras, red bud, sugar maple, sycamore, cottonwood, beech, buckeye, and locust. The beauty that is left is still the profusion of trees although lightning and windstorm have taken their toll. It was Hall who wrote: "The magnificent forest trees attained a gigantic height." The spot remains a woodland, and it is fitting that the early pioneers who died in Vandalia remain on this scenic knoll. It seems ill-fated that Hall, who earned a final resting place in a picturesque woodland area which he so zealously recounted to others, was not buried here. Nonetheless the Hall name is held in memory through his wife and infant son.

As the visitor proceeds south of Mary Hall's grave, he finds the monument of James W. Berry, the distinguished artist who selected subjects from his own town and on his canvas gave them character, verity, and energy. A well-turned epitaph should have been inscribed upon the artist's monument in honor of the painter who could express so well the features of men on canvas. Perhaps a belated epitaph, although it is inadequate, might help in serving to immortalize his name:

> Farewell, pioneer painter
> With a noble heart!
> Your memory grows fainter
> But not your art.
> James Berry, you have
> Acted well your part .

As the visitor leaves the Berry monument, he may turn to the pathway, proceed about ten feet, and view the Ferdinand Ernst monument at his left. One will observe by the inscriptions on the markers that some died very young. Conditions were not so healthful in this newly settled prairie region. An epidemic of malarial diseases caused the deaths of numerous members of the Hanover Colony including the leader, Ferdinand Ernst. In 1823 many communities in the Ohio Valley were affected by the ravages of ague, typhoid, and other malarial diseases.

Near the Ernst marker is that of Robert Blackwell, first public printer in Illinois. Across the pathway the William C. Greenup tombstone marks the grave of the capital surveyor. In the northwest corner of the burial ground one can view the McLaughlin monument. It seems that visitors know very little about the first state treasurer in Vandalia. Robert K. McLaughlin brought with him from Kaskaskia the first slaves to live in Fayette County. Born in Virginia in 1779, he early acquired the qualities of hospitality, kindness, and courtesy for which his fellow-Virginians were noted in early days. He emigrated to Kentucky and then settled in Illinois in 1815. The family of five Negroes whom he brought with him to Vandalia soon ran away, but he made no effort to find them. In his wife's will a sufficient amount of money was left to provide for her Negro servant Mary Ann until her death. Perhaps not all ran away.

After having entered the legal profession, Robert McLaughlin occupied several important government posts. He served as state treasurer from 1819-1823 under Governor Bond. Later he served in both the House of Representatives and in the Senate. After the removal of the capital to Springfield, McLaughlin devoted his energies to the growth of the Vandalia community in which he became an eminent citizen of considerable wealth. From 1837-1845 he was registrar of the General Land Office in Vandalia.

A letter, written by McLaughlin petitioning the General Assembly to reimburse him for firewood and candles which he used during the winter of 1820-21 in his house, testifies to the fact that his home was used for the treasurer's office. He had not received compensation from the state as others who had used their houses for offices. He requested the "honorable body" to allow him the sum that was honestly due him.

Since his wife's uncle Shadrach Bond resided with them during his term as governor, the McLaughlin residence was referred to as the governor's mansion. Little can be found that has been recorded by contemporaries about this house. In a codicil to Isabella McLaughlin's will on February 25, 1867, she states:

> And the property described in lines 24, 25 and 26 numbering from the top of said will as "My old homestead house and orchard in North Square Vandalia, Illinois" is the lot next west of the Presbyterian Church where my dwelling now stands and that portion of the north part of the Presbyterian Church, lot and also that lying north of my dwelling house lot and now used by me as a garden and orchard.[5]

Original Buildings and Places

The McLaughlin residence was quite the social center where the most fashionable and prominent people of the day gathered. Robert and Isabella McLaughlin were perhaps the most popular and most esteemed couple in the capital. When a group of men wrote the *History of Fayette County, Illinois* in 1878, they recorded of this couple: "Their bodies repose in the Cemetery in Vandalia, but their memories are still living and will continue to live so long as genius and goodness are esteemed desirable attributes."[6] For the most part their memory has slipped into oblivion except for the octagonal shaft which stands on a square base bearing the inscription of McLaughlin's birth and death dates (1779-1862) and his wife's (1791-1868).

The ancient village is not forgetful of its war dead. Not far from the McLaughlin monument level with the ground is a small white slab (10 x 8 inches) on which are engraved the words: *Gustav Stahl, Blockade runner of Vicksburg.* Although no impressive monument marks his memory, the visitor realizes that no matter how small a part one played he is recognized for giving his last full measure of devotion to his country. If the visitor takes a guided tour through the graveyard, the guide will show him the slab and at the same time remind him that the Mississippi River was a vital lifeline to the Confederates and that Vicksburg was the key to its control. It has been said that President Lincoln remarked that he wanted that key to put in his pocket in order to bring the war to an end. Gustav Stahl helped his commander-in-chief to gain possession of that important item.

The most dramatic story of the graveyard is told by the white column marking Colonel Lucian Greathouse's remains. The impressive inscription pays tribute to the brave young colonel who led his command in forty-one battles. The epitaph, although not written by a Shelley or a Milton, is nonetheless a striking account of a courageous youth who played his part in maintaining that a group of states could not be larger than the Union. On the tombstone one discovers that Colonel Greathouse was killed at the head of his regiment before Atlanta, Georgia, July 22, 1864, at the age of twenty-two years. He served under the distinguished General William Sherman who said of Greathouse: "His example was worth a thousand men." General John A. Logan, the valorous volunteer soldier of Illinois, extolled: "The bravest man in the army of the Tennessee."

47

Colonel Greathouse fought in the battles of Fort Henry and Fort Donaldson, the capture of which laid open the valleys of both the Tennessee and Cumberland Rivers to the Union Army. He fought with the forces at Shiloh and Corinth. He was with Sherman assaulting the bluffs above Vicksburg. Again he was with him at the capture of Chattanooga, at the battles of Lookout Mountain, Mission Ridge, Altoona Pass, and Kenesaw Mountain. Then came the arduous task of the Atlanta campaign to which Sherman set himself. The Confederates gathered every soldier they could spare to guard the country between Chattanooga and Atlanta. The courage and discipline of the commanders and the soldiers of the Union Army were magnificent. Although the mountains were crowned with heavy artillery and the advance on that line almost impossible, the skill of Sherman and the Union commanders compelled the Confederates to retreat from one position to another. When the Union Army was approaching Atlanta to destroy the only manufacturing town of importance, Colonel Greathouse lost his life carrying the flag of his regiment and his country in hand standing upon the breastworks of the enemy. It seems significant that Vandalia's Civil War hero gave his life for the principles that Lincoln stood for as a young legislator in the pioneer Illinois capital.

THE COTTAGE BELIEVED TO HAVE BEEN LINCOLN'S LODGING

History haunts a prim little cottage which stands west of the Baptist Church between Sixth and Seventh Streets. The white-painted dwelling whose address is 615 West Johnson reminds one of the Bryant House at Bement where Lincoln and Douglas are supposed to have made their agreement to debate. It is also similar to the John Deere House at Grand Detour. It has been reported since capital days that the humble dwelling sheltered Lincoln for one legislative session. He took his rest in the simple southwest room of the house that has stood as a landmark in Vandalia's history.

Mrs. John Van Dorsten, who entertained General John A. Logan in her home on the northeast corner of Sixth and Edwards Streets, maintained that the cottage served as Lincoln's lodging for one session of the legislature. Older residents have forgotten the exact term but recall the account that Lincoln rented a room in the cottage. Mrs. Van Dorsten is the one who protested the account of Lafayette's visit to Vandalia. Historians as far back as 1878 have claimed that the French general paid a visit to the capital in 1825. Mrs. Van Dorsten disagreed with the statement every time that she found it. But she persisted in the belief that Lincoln rented a room in the cottage. No doubt she had substantial reasons for her belief. Indeed Lincoln lived some place during the years 1834-1839. Older citizens have maintained that this cottage holds memories close to its wooden heart about the immortal Lincoln.

LINCOLN COTTAGE

When the author inquired of one Vandalian whether or not he had heard that Lincoln lived there, he answered without hesitation, "Yes, Lincoln stayed there." He had not only heard of Mrs. Van Dorsten's account, but he was present when Tillie Ernst, the grand-daughter of the leader of the Hanover Colony, told his mother that Lincoln rented a room in the cottage. "That confirms it, doesn't it?" [7] The author of this book needs no further substantiation of the oral record.

The gable-roofed cottage has undergone a modicum of remodeling at which time the two rooms in the rear were partitioned, its old windows were removed, and two rooms were added. The old windows still remain at the front and on the west side. No doubt the front door is original since houses built in the 1830's often possess this type of architectural design. It is quite simply constructed with many-paned windows, and although the timber appears aged, the house has remained in fairly good condition. The one-story dwelling with its white picket fence has not been set apart to the memory of the young legislator, but later generations have not allowed to die the report that Lincoln at one time occupied the cottage.

THE COUNCIL TREE

The mammoth cottonwood tree which still stands on the Clark property at the rear of the old house was used as a council tree by five major Indian tribes of the Midwest according to oral tradition. Daniel M. Clark reported that the tribes met annually for a powwow under the spreading cottonwood. It was a geographic landmark on a promontory where nothing obstructed the view of the river and surrounding area. The Council Tree was also used as a lookout. The lithe-limbed Indians climbed the tree in order to survey the area which was a central place for a powwow. [8]

It was a typical practice among Indians to gather for a conference with other tribes to settle disputes or to arrange for designating certain areas to be used for hunting and fishing by the tribes. The stretch of country where Vandalia is located was apparently not densely populated with savages. Their occupancy of this land seemed to be periodic. The Council Tree is located one block east of the State Burial Ground. Since the cottonwood stands on a high point of land overlooking the Kaskaskia River, no doubt the Indians traveled by canoe to attend the powwow. One can almost visualize the gathering of the redmen as he views the majestic cottonwood and other large trees on the Clark acreage.

THE BLACKWELL PRINTERY

From the little wooden structure that still stands today issued forth a record that ought not be neglected in relating events that occurred over one hundred and forty years ago. One must be mindful of the fact that the contemporary traveler to Vandalia observed only a small part of a frontier community. Likewise, the pioneer on the scene also selected events and scenery that interested him. But in the Blackwell Printery a newspaper and a magazine recorded events as the capital contemporaries saw them without the distorting medium of later knowledge.

When Robert Blackwell moved from the territorial capital, Kaskaskia, to Vandalia, he brought with him a printing press. Whether or not it was the hand press developed in the early 1800's is not known. But he established at the new capital a printing plant in a two-story frame building which was soon to be known as the Blackwell Printery. It was originally located the second door west of the present building on the southwest corner of Gallatin and Fourth Streets (it can be viewed on the mural painting at Hotel Evans for a better idea of its location). The Blackwell Printery has been moved to a less prominent spot on the northwest corner of Jefferson and Second Streets where few people are cognizant of its memorable past. Rarely does one point with pride at the historic little printery that was actually the first center of literary activity in the state of Illinois. It has undergone remodeling but substantially it exists very nearly as it did in 1830 when James Hall insured its interest and its fame to posterity upon the publication of his *Illinois Monthly Magazine*.

Robert Blackwell came as the state printer to the new capital and retained that position until 1832. He derived his most dependable income from government printing contracts; both advertising and subscriptions were uncertain sources of income. His editorship of the Illinois *Intelligencer*, the most influential and noteworthy newspaper in the state, was periodic but nevertheless substantial. From 1832-1836 Blackwell was a member of the House of Representatives, and from 1838-1840 he served as state senator.

In 1823 when William Berry, the uncle of the artist James Berry, was his co-editor, Robert Blackwell took up the cause of the convention since he had always held pro-slavery sentiments. It must be noted, however, that Robert Blackwell strongly believed in the freedom of the press. When Governor Coles purchased the *Intelligencer* and David Blackwell replaced his brother as editor, the newspaper became an opponent of the convention. By examining the files one is well aware that the newspaper served as a political organ on the frontier. The procedure of acquiring the newspaper was considered good politics; its effect upon the freedom of the press did not concern Coles as much as the preservation of human freedom. The little printery bustled with activity; the press denounced slavery, declaring it contrary to the principles of the Declaration of Independence. It insisted slavery was a moral issue. Indeed the opponents of Governor Coles were confronted by forceful and enthusiastic writers. Morris Birkbeck, "a man trained in the principles of human liberty, intellectually the descendant of well-nigh six generations of radicals who labored for the people's freedom," [9] raised the most convincing arguments against the convention. Indeed the newspaper wielded a tremendous influence in heated controversies as well as political campaigns.

As one peruses the files of the Illinois *Intelligencer*, he is acutely aware of the bondage of human beings. Notices of rewards for runaway slaves appeared frequently. One notice of a "runaway taken up" in the newspaper for Saturday, November 16, 1822 reads:

> Runaway taken up And committed to my custody on the 17th of this month, a bright mulatto man who calls himself Jonathan Ward, about 5 feet 8 or 9 inches high, well made, and appears to be about 26 or 27 years of age, blue eyes, speaks with confidence; he has passed in this place for six or eight weeks as a free man. The owner would do well to come forward, prove property, pay charges, and take him away.
>
> Jos. Oliver
Sheriff of Fayette County
>
> Vandalia, Illinois   Oct. 17, 1822

More attention is given to literary pursuits than one might think in an age when editors struggled with problems created by difficulties of communication. The interest in a new novel which later become a part of the American literary heritage credits the editors' judgment. On the third page of the *Intelligencer* Thursday, June 29, 1826, appeared the brief article:

> *Literary*—Messrs. Cary and Lee, of Philadelphia, are about to publish a new novel from the pen of the American novelist, Mr. Cooper, entitled the *Prairie*. Mr. Cooper's standing and former productions will ensure for this work a favorable reception, and we doubt not the *Prairie* will issue from the press as interesting in fiction as it is agreeable in reality.

The news at the capital emerged from the printery on varied subjects that now belong to the history of American civilization. John T. Flanagan, professor of English at the University of Illinois and author of the only definitive biography of James Hall, has adequately and concisely presented a resumé of the contents of the *Intelligencer* in a paper entitled "James Hall, Pioneer Vandalia Editor and Publicist," which he delivered at the annual meeting of the Illinois State Historical Society in Vandalia on October 8, 1954. The paper also gives in a direct and energetic style an impressive delineation of the editor.

The Blackwell Printery gained its first recognition in housing the most prominent newspaper in Illinois. But it became richer in significance when James Hall seized upon the idea of publishing a literary magazine which had no equal in the whole history of the frontier. For it was James Hall, a Philadelphian by birth and a lawyer by profession, who brought to the wilderness capital its distinction—the first center of literary activity in the state of Illinois. Hall, the state treasurer, not finding his life swallowed up by official duties, purchased in January, 1829, a half interest in the *Intelligencer*, which under his editorship with his co-owner Robert Blackwell, continued to be an outstanding newspaper.

An increased interest in the subject of literature became noticeable in the paper after Hall began his editorship. The February 21, 1829 issue contained a poem from the *Western Souvenir* under a section entitled *Poetry*. In the lyric "To Mary" Hall has immortalized his wife showing both his fluency and skill in versification:

> My Mary, if the tales were true,
>   Of fairy forms they tell,
> Who sip from flowers the balmy dew,
>   Or haunt the shadowy dell:
> Who watch the silent glance or tear,
>   What bashful maids conceal
> And softly to the enamoured dear,
>   The tender tale reveal;
>
> How blest would be the rapid wing
>   Of herald true as these;
> Soft messages of love to bring,
>   Swift as the sweeping breeze;

> For they to thee would whisper, dear,
>   Of him far from thee driven,
> Whose sighs ascend in daily prayer,
>   For thy dear sake to heaven!
>
> And, Mary! they would softly tell,
>   Where 'er I chanced to rove,
> What anxious thoughts my bosom swell,
>   For thee—my plighted love!
> And daily when thy cheeks reveal
>   Charms so divine in thee,
> Soft kisses, they would gently steal,
>   And bear the sweets to me.

Although Hall was delicate in expressing the feelings of his heart, he was vigorous and aggressive in his editorials. A contemporary J. M. Duncan, brother of Governor Duncan, refers to Hall as a "talented editor" in a letter to Senator Kane February 25, 1830: "Judge Hall, the Editor of the paper at this place, as you (will) see, by the paper, made a bold, able, and decisive stand in favour of yourself and the rest of our friends—The Extensive circulation of this paper will give its talented editor an excellent opportunity of exposing the machinations of the designing men . . . ." [10] Indeed, there was great excitement in the frontier printery during the gubernatorial election of 1830. Hall vigorously supported William Kinney and to use the colorful phrasing of John T. Flanagan "the *Intelligencer* shot forth many an arrow in his cause as Hall entered the fray with the vehemence of a gladiator." [11] John Reynolds, the opposing candidate, was aware of the force and influence of this fiery editor.

In that same year Hall launched into his really daring venture— editing a literary periodical in the wilderness where drinking, gambling, and fighting prevailed among the frontier element and where literary tastes had not been in a general sense established in the new state. Robert Blackwell would print the periodical, for was not this little spot on the Kaskaskia River a veritable nest for teaching fledglings to try their wings? Blackwell realized that Hall had created quite an impression with his editorship of the *Intelligencer* and *Western Souvenir*. He had already earned the reputation of being one of the most prolific and forceful writers on the frontier after his publication of *Letters from the West*. Soon Blackwell was setting his movable type, and within a short period literary activity prevailed. Since the printery was established as the first literary center in Illinois, it is appropriate in these pages to emphasize the fact that Hall was strengthening his niche in American letters at this historic place although it is necessary to examine his activity in a separate chapter.

At his desk in the printery Hall was eager to record the legends which he had heard at the firesides in Vandalia. How many hours he spent in the printery assembling the tales cannot be ascertained. The pioneers welcomed good story-tellers at the cabin firesides, in the capital inns, or around campfires. Hall saw entertaining material and humor in the dramatic and colorful personalities of the legends. He quickly captured the versions of this oral literature, for in them he saw the American spirit expressing itself in subject matter that was unmistakably American. When he was not writing editorials, he recorded the folklore he had heard. Indeed, the vitality of his sketches of frontier life that emerged from the Blackwell Printery secured for Hall a place in any survey of fiction or record of history in American literature; likewise, the Blackwell Printery ought to have its security among the literary shrines of America. Unfortunately, it has no distinctive features of architecture. It is a frontier printery unimpressive for its appearance but highly impressive for its literary past!

THE VANDALIA STATEHOUSE

Out of this brick and wood
From its base to its cupola
Thou, Lincoln, learned to lead the world.
Thy wise soul belongs to all the world—
To Europe, to Asia, to Africa!
Thou art the great emancipator
For all mankind.

Swayed by Jefferson's Declaration
And poised by a freedom-loving soul,
Thou protested the injustices of slavery
Opposing thy learned colleagues
Within these venerable walls.
Abraham Lincoln, steady, daring youth,
Here rises thy true monument!

Vandalia: Wilderness Capital of Lincoln's Land

THE OLD STATEHOUSE

Vandalia's greatest link with the past is the impressive State-house, built in 1836 by the townspeople to retain the capital. It addresses itself to the imagination of visitors and has endeared itself to the great American nation. On its register is a host of visitors' names from Europe and Asia as well as the United States. The old edifice, a symbol of American liberty and a shrine to perpetuate Abraham Lincoln's memory, has a beauty touched with simplicity and pioneer charm. So solidly and firmly it stands in the memory of the glory it has known. The venerable building is too wise to boast, but it shows a pride in the fact that a great American president began his political career in Vandalia, and for three years of that period it served to house the legislative sessions that Lincoln attended.

Visitors seem to revere its lawmaking role in the life of the early pioneers and the fact that the Statehouse identifies itself with the wise and understanding man who believed in the great truths of the Declaration of Independence. For here, Lincoln, stirred by the thoughts and plans of zealous legislators, developed into a patriot and statesman who was later to become chief executive of the nation. It was here that Lincoln learned the art of government. Always sensitive to human rights, the young inexperienced lawmaker acquired the basic foundations of governmental practices when he represented the people of Sangamon County. The Statehouse, then, is the most important edifice in the old capital. Although totally lacking in ornate decoration, it asserts its majesty and makes one sense it. It is nothing to excite wonder but its very simplicity pleases. Today it is chiefly a place of pilgrimage for those who pay tribute to the memory of Abraham Lincoln and other illustrious statesmen who served here.

The Statehouse is the third one in Vandalia. The first frame capitol burned in December, 1823, and the citizens, eager to provide quarters for the capitol, built a two-story brick building on the site of the Hotel Evans dining room. It was demolished in 1836, and some of its brick and wood were used to erect the capitol which now stands on the square. The Vandalia citizens, hoping to keep the seat of government, spent $16,000 to construct a capitol. John Taylor and William Hodge drew the plans for the two-story structure. Levi Davis, A. P. Field, and James T. B. Stapp headed the movement to finance the fund to erect the Statehouse. The Tenth General Assembly convened December 5, 1836, in the new capitol although much remained to be done within the structure. Eight days later Lincoln in his letter to Mary Owens wrote: "The new State House is not yet finished, and consequently the legislature is doing little or nothing." [12] After the legislature had passed the bill to remove the capital to Springfield, the lawmakers voted to refund to Vandalia the amount expended for construction of the Statehouse.

There was little in the way of adornment until the eight Doric piers (the four brick columns on each portico) were erected in 1859. Rexford Newcomb, who has studied various aspects of architectural expression in the Midwest, says:

> The Vandalia Capitol, now restored as a state monument, presents a two-story Greek-temple mass of white-painted brick. The interior is quartered by corridors, the principal entrances opening upon porticos which flank the long sides of the building. Each of these porticos has four Doric piers supporting a light pediment. Atop the roof stands an octagonal lantern, which is perhaps more Federal than Greek in spirit. The doorways show the typical treatment with transom and side lights, and the windows are appropriately framed. [13]

After the removal of the capital in 1839, Vandalia withered like a prairie flower in the heat and did not survive until the Illinois Central in the 1850's sent its railroad through the town. During the decade following the capital period the population was sparse. There must not have been more than three hundred people residing in the neglected town. In 1839 the State of Illinois donated the old capitol to Fayette County for courthouse purposes. It seems that only the west portion of the building was occupied. The use of the east half of the building is somewhat uncertain. The upper east room was turned into a school. According to some reports, the east half was soon in a ruinous condition. The winds whistled through the glassless window frames in the rooms not in use. The animals roamed at large through the wide halls. The saddened scene must have made the patriots weep. But when the county purchased the east portion of the Statehouse from the Fayette Seminary, it renovated the venerable building and kept it in good repair.

Today the Statehouse stands as a memorial to the early pioneers of Illinois. It is comprised of four large rooms and a spacious foyer on the ground floor. The east side housed the Supreme Court and the Secretary of State. The west wing comprised the Auditor of Public Accounts and the State Treasurer's offices. The upper floor contains the Senate Chamber, Hall of Representatives, and the Governor's office or committee room (it was frequently used for this purpose). The rooms have been restored by using original furniture and reproductions designed according to that period. Various items are placed in the rooms in order to create frontier atmosphere. This was the day of resourceful pioneers. Sand was used for plotting. Quill pens are on the desks. Woodboxes in each room indicate that timber provided the source of fuel.

The southeast room which housed the Supreme Court of Illinois is the most famous one on the lower floor. On a raised dais four high-back chairs face the chamber which is furnished with simple benches and small primitive desks. Here the visitor often feels himself profoundly moved, for in this room which is quiet and solemn with tradition, a twenty-eight-year-old legislator on a March day in 1837 received his permission to execute the duties of attorney and counselor at law. That young man was Abraham Lincoln.

It was here that Samuel Drake Lockwood, the noted jurist, served as judge of the Supreme Court of Illinois. He was one of the few lawyers who acted in behalf of the anti-slavery cause in the years 1822-1824. So many influential ones were either from the slave states or pro-slavery in their sentiments. Justice Lockwood served in the chamber of the Supreme Court three of his years (1836-1839) on the bench. In Vandalia he also was appointed attorney general by the legislature and was appointed secretary of state before his election as an associate justice.

Judge Lockwood devoted his skill and talents to this branch of government and achieved distinction in his responsibility toward his judicial duties. As a lawyer and judge his work was characterized by wisdom, intelligence, and integrity. Probably his most notable single contribution was the revision of the state statutes. One may assume from the historical records of Vandalia that Lockwood was beloved and respected as probably no other magistrate in Illinois.

It is well to mention at this point the chief-justice, William Wilson, who presided at the bench from 1825-1848. It appears according to the records that he demonstrated prudence and a conscientious attitude in court decisions and that he stood apart from political maneuvering. In his efforts, furthermore, he put a personal stamp on cultural activities in the capital; to mention only one, he served as vice-president of the first historical society in Illinois. So the chamber is famous for the judges who performed their duties here as well as for a young man who received permission to practice law.

As the spell of the ancient room is settling upon the visitor,—for very likely he is impressed with the sense of solemn trusts confided to the wisdom of the justices—a guide may invite his attention to a little village located in the northeastern part of Illinois during the capital period. This small settlement of log huts was receiving food supplies from Kaskaskia during the 1820's. Ten years later it consisted of some fifty clapboard houses. But the village was growing; newcomers were swarming into the settlement. In the winter of 1835-1836 the legislature passed the act authorizing the canal, and when the actual digging began, still larger groups of people came to the village. [14] In 1837 in the chamber of the Supreme Court, Chicago was granted its charter to become a city. Some Chicagoans are swept with sudden amazement upon hearing that their charter was obtained from this old town which is often unknown to them until their current visit.

A. P. Field, secretary of state, held his office in the northeast room, which contains Governor Reynolds' distinctive cherry desk and quaint pewter candlesticks. In the cherished relic have been placed books published during capital days. Especially interesting is an original copy of *Reports of Cases at Common Law* (1831) by Sidney Breese. It is appropriate for the desk to remain in the room where Reynolds' friend performed his duties as state secretary.

In the northwest room a likeness of Levi Davis, who served as auditor of public accounts in the Statehouse, hangs on the wall. In the southwest room across the hall the state treasurers served— Charles Gregory of Greene County and John Whiteside of Monroe; the former served only three months. A large desk of handsome wood and attractive design is said to have been there during capital days. According to the original detail plan the southwest room served as the office of the secretary of state. The northeast room was the treasurer's office. When the Statehouse was restored, the rooms were identified differently from that of the supposedly original plan.

Ascending the ancient stairway, one recalls the legend about Douglas riding a donkey up the steps to celebrate a democratic victory. At the top of the stairway one sees the governor's office or committee room where Lincoln often served on various committees. Again one is uncertain as to the use of the large rooms on the upper floor. Prior to the restoration the west room had always been referred to as the House of Representatives. Capital descendants had been informed by their ancestors of this identification. The east room had been called the Senate Chamber. According to the original detail plan those designations are accurate. After the restoration the rooms were labeled differently. The spectators galleries have not been restored. Originally they projected into both the Senate Chamber and Hall of Representatives.

The favored historical item is the original key which still opens the massive doors. After July 4, 1839, the regency of the old edifice was resigned to Vandalia. Dr. A. L. T. Williams for many years guarded the key from loss. Who had protected its safety prior to that time is not known by the author. Dr. Williams asked Mrs. Eualia Smith Perkins to guard the hereditary possession. She gladly accepted the trust. After Joseph Burtschi, as the agent of Fayette County, had negotiated the sale of the Statehouse with Governor Frank Lowden, Mrs. Perkins then presented the key to the director of public parks. He, in turn, used it as a model from which to pattern other keys for the Statehouse doors. [15]

The Statehouse has undergone little change in appearance as compared to other original buildings. From 1858-1859 the county added porticoes supported by massive Doric piers to both the north and south sides and rearranged the interior. In 1889 the brick columns were replaced by iron pillars, and a balcony was added. In 1930 the cupola was entirely destroyed by fire, and the six-foot metal weather vane was crumpled during the blaze to such an extent that it had to be replaced. The state architects by examining old photographs rebuilt the cupola.

In 1933 when Fayette County moved its offices into another building, the state began to restore the old capitol. The policy was established after a number of consultations to recreate the interior visual surfaces and to retain the 1858 exterior appearance. In 1936 Illinois was granted funds from the Federal Government for the project, and the interior of the building regained its original appearance by 1938. The state then obtained funds for the exterior work in 1939. The iron pillars and balcony were removed, and brick Doric piers were built. Since the cupola was incorrectly designed in 1930, it was rebuilt. The restoration of the exterior was finished in 1940. The diamond-shaped pathway circumscribing the structure and four walks leading from it were retained. The Madonna of the Trail Statue was moved from the front entrance to the southwest corner of the square. Plans were then made to place furniture of the capital period in the rooms; unfortunately, at this writing the project has not been completed although some furnishings are there. Two rooms have been completely restored.

Record of the Restoration of the Third Statehouse, Vandalia, Illinois, 1930-1945 by Joseph Booten and George Nedved is a 125-page booklet which covers the history of this building in chronological order. The research treatise at the beginning was concerned with the furniture and furnishings of the structure, but later the architects decided to enlarge its scope by including a complete record of the edifice.

Drawings of tools and equipment, especially ink-wells and wood sandboxes, used by persons employed in the Statehouse are included. It was apparently the practice to blot the wet ink on a written page by sprinkling a fine sand on it. Sandboxes now appear in the various rooms. The sandbox is not to be confused with the spitbox or spittoon which was filled with sawdust or sand. Photographs of heating-stoves, tin and candle lamps, tin wall sconces, bookcases, desks, and chairs are also included. Similar furnishings now appear in the various rooms. The architects mention, too, the fact that the stairhall is off axis of the center of the building; the rooms on the east side are larger than those on the west. The list of salaries and wages paid in 1836 is another interesting part of the research. The governor received an annual salary of $1,000; the secretary of state, $600; the auditor of public accounts, $700; and the treasurer, $500. The salary of a legislator per day was $4 plus travel expenses ($4 per 20 miles). A

Vandalia: Wilderness Capital of Lincoln's Land

laborer for digging dirt to lay the foundation of the capitol was paid $1 a day. The night watchman for the Statehouse received $2.75 per week. Indeed this research treatise is an adequate and valuable record of the Statehouse.

Visitors to the Statehouse frequently inquire about Lincoln's jump. According to one story, Lincoln was present at a night meeting of the legislators in the southwest room. The exact proportion of members with a preponderance of Vandalia supporters was present to vote on the removal of the capital. In order to break the quorum, Lincoln jumped out the window. He swung himself over the ledge and landed on the ground. Another version holds that the meeting took place during the day in the House of Representatives. Although Lincoln was an agile, tall young man, it is difficult to conceive of his jumping out the second-story window. The legend was fated to perish long ago, but it is still commonly referred to by visitors.

Such is the history of this venerable building which is a reminder of a former age when famous statesmen assembled in the old rooms and walked through the corridors. Many are the hallowed associations that can be revived in the visitor's mind. When Ida Tarbell reported her pilgrimage to Vandalia, she said that the town "had unmistakable distinction" during capital days because of the men who dominated it. These men "of fine caliber" were an "exciting change" to the young Lincoln, who had known no such "animated social life."[16] The impressive capitol reminds visitors not only of Lincoln but of those determined pioneers who operated a government in the wilderness. Visitors are disposed to grateful feelings that the Statehouse is carefully preserved in remembrance of old times.

ORIGINAL BUILDINGS AND PLACES
1. Brink, McDonough & Co., op. cit., p. 29
2. Marguerite Pease, **Guide to Manuscript Materials of American Origin in the Illinois Historical Survey** (Urbana, 1956), p. 29. The letter does not appear in the publication but is a listed item in the Illinois Historical Survey.
3. Burtschi, **op. cit.,** p. 80
4. Mrs. Maude Bradley Bellechamber by interview supplied the information. Le Grand Flack substantiated the report.
5. Burtschi Bros. & Co., **Abstract Copybook** #64, p. 692
6. Brink and McDonough, op. cit., p. 29
7. Christian Janett by interview supplied the information.
8. Misses Sally and Ethel Clark, granddaughters of Daniel Clark, supplied the information by interview.
9. Pease, **The Frontier State,** p. 87
10. Chicago Historical Society, Kane MSS., Vol. LIII. The transcripts were used in the Illinois Historical Survey, Urbana.
11. J. T. Flanagan, **James Hall, Literary Pioneer of the Ohio Valley** (Minneapolis, 1941), p. 47
12. Carl Sandburg, **Abraham Lincoln: The Prairie Years,** Vol. I (New York, 1941), p. 203
13. Rexford Newcomb, **Architecture of the Old Northwest Territory** (Chicago, 1950), p. 102
14. W. L. Nida, **The Story of Illinois and Its People** (Chicago, 1923), pp. 143-146
15. Information obtained from Mrs. Ben Perkins by interview.
16. Ida M. Tarbell, **In the Footsteps of the Lincolns** (New York, 1924), pp. 205-206

ABRAHAM LINCOLN AND OTHER
PERSONALITIES

The history of Vandalia is quite arresting when one studies the lives of the men who labored so vigorously that a democratic commonwealth be established in the wilderness of a new state. The history of America is so vitally interesting because of the really colorful personalities that figure in it. The ideas they were putting into governmental action are still so living. Gilbert K. Chesterton says in the essay "On America" that the history of the United States "is one of the most picturesque and personal of all the histories of the nations. The number of really interesting characters that figure in it is very large. The ideas and ideals for which they stood are very living." [1]

Indeed this little spot on the Kaskaskia River drew its share of romantic figures. One became capable of filling the highest office in the United States with honor and success. Possibly Lincoln, not living with these patriots, would have had his light quenched in the general dimness that surrounded him in New Salem (his trysts for learning with Mentor Graham and Jack Kelso were exceptions). Stephen Douglas, the Democratic presidential candidate opposing Lincoln in 1860, came at the age of twenty-one to Vandalia where he met Lincoln for the first time. Douglas was an impressive figure in the state government; he became such on the national scene, too. Other legislators like Browning, Baker, and Kane afterwards played important roles in the nation's history.

The success of these statesmen in laying the democratic foundations for the state was not phenomenal, for they had a keen sense of what to do. They were equipped with the drive and intellect to succeed in working out the conception of democracy. They, on the whole, realized their opportunities of freedom and did not fail to think deeply about the problems that affected their lives and their safety. The question of internal improvements was a practical problem which they met with a lesser degree of favorable result than the others. Educating the populace through public funds was a real problem. The equality of man and his right to pursue happiness as a free individual was a very pressing one. The anti-slavery elements protested vigorously infringement upon the principle of the rights of man. The success of the banking system meant a strong economic growth; the failure meant disaster to the general public.

The reader dislikes to be whisked from one subject to another so that the sketch of each personality blurs rather than clarifies. It is hoped that the brevity of treatment will not create indistinctness. These biographical vignettes serve the purpose of emphasizing the fact that Lincoln and Douglas were not the only captivating figures in Vandalia. Since James Hall was conspicuously successful in his writing efforts at Vandalia, his biography and activities merit a separate chapter. The men who practiced their political craft in the early capital gained ideas and experiences that carried them into national endeavors which helped to make this country the great nation it is today.

EDWARD DICKINSON BAKER

An important political personality in the United States during Lincoln's presidency was Edward Dickinson Baker. He first met the prairie lawyer at Springfield where Baker came to live in 1835. Baker was born in London, England, February 24, 1811. He emigrated at the age of five to the United States with his parents and older brother Alfred. The family first lived in New Harmony, Indiana, for a short period of time; they then moved to Belleville and later to Carrolton in Illinois. At twenty-four Baker decided to move his wife and children to Springfield, a rapidly growing town. In March, 1837, Lincoln was returning on the stage coach with the rest of the Sangamon delegation in great triumph; this group of lawmakers had been successful in passing the bill to move the capital to Springfield. Soon the young, English-born political aspirant would be joining Lincoln on the stage back to Vandalia (it remained the capital until 1839). Dan Stone, a Sangamon County representative, had resigned his position to become judge. A special election to fill the vacancy took place. Baker was chosen for the seat. On July 4, 1837, Springfield observed the customary celebration with an added excitement. It was the cornerstone laying of the new statehouse; Baker accepted the invitation to be the principal speaker for the occasion.

Almost a week later, Baker took his place at the famous Tenth General Assembly. In fact, on the opening day, July 10, he with Dawson and Elkin was one of only three Sangamon representatives. Lincoln and Edwards were in their seats the next day. The others came later in the week.[2] It was the Englishman's first time to serve in a legislature. Four days after the convening of the assembly Baker received an appointment to a committee on which Abraham Lincoln and Ninian Edwards, son of the third governor, also served. The purpose of the committee was to consider a bill to extend the corporate powers of the town Springfield.[3]

Excitement was high in the capital! General Ewing had announced that he intended to introduce a bill to repeal laws relative to the location of the seat of government. It appeared that Springfield might not be the permanent capital if Usher Linder, an anti-bank lobbyist, or Alec Field or Robert McLaughlin or any pro-Vandalia men would seize a chance to outwit the opposition. Indeed they were fighting with vigor to retain the capital. Every stratagem presented to them they employed. Lincoln and the Sangamon County men also appeared insensible to any other situation that needed their attention in the legislature. Governor Duncan was attempting to point out to the lawmakers the folly of the internal improvement program. Had not millions of state funds been spent for no purpose? But the legislators continued to squabble about the capital relocation.

In 1838 Baker again returned to Vandalia as a Whig representative in the Eleventh General Assembly. Here, like Lincoln, he was learning governmental practices. He was definitely in the contest for political honors in the state; he was enterprising, ambitious, and able. Lincoln was becoming a closer personal friend to him.

After Baker left Vandalia, he distinguished himself as a Mexican War soldier when he won recognition as a hero in the battle of Cerro Gordo, as a prominent United States Senator from Oregon, and as a Civil War colonel who died in 1861 on the battlefield. When the news of Baker's death reached the White House, both President Lincoln and his wife grieved at the loss of a close friend. Memorial services were held for Baker in the Senate Chambers where President Lincoln attended to pay tribute to a loyal personal friend, a competent senator, and a truly good American who served his country well in his devotion to freedom.

JAMES W. BERRY

So little is recorded of this early American painter that one making an effort to seek knowledge concerning his birth and death would be able to find it in the old State Burial Ground in Vandalia where Berry's marker states that he was born July 16, 1805 and died January 7, 1877. The other two names on the monument belong to his parents, Elijah Conway and Mildred Stapp Berry.

In 1819 Elijah C. Berry with his wife, a large family of children, and a family of Negro slaves (they remained with him and his descendants until death) moved from Kaskaskia to the new capital. Elijah served as auditor of public accounts for the state from 1819-1831. He was elected president of the old State Bank of Vandalia in 1837. The Berrys lived in comfortable circumstances; high ideals, integrity, refinement, and industry were a natural part of their background. Little is known about the education of James. According to a letter written by Eleanor Field to her father, Melinda Berry, James' sister, attended Ménard Academy in Kaskaskia. Whether or not Elijah provided educational advantages for all his children is a matter of conjecture. If he were unable to give his son college training, it is no discredit to him, for even some of the most capable men who came to Vandalia did not possess a formal education.

At the age of twenty-one James Berry became circuit clerk of Fayette County and competently served in that position for thirty years. During that time he was active in community affairs. He served as adjutant-general from December 19, 1828, until he resigned November 11, 1839. In 1835 the legislature passed an act in which Berry, along with Harvey Lee and Joseph Eccles, was appointed commissioner to lay off one-half acre of the graveyard to be used for the burial of members of the Senate and House of Representatives and other governmental officers who would die in the discharge of their duties. He was further commissioned to enclose the one-half acre with a strong, substantial fence. The sum was not to exceed fifty dollars. Then in 1840 when a covered bridge was to be built by the United States Government across the Kaskaskia River on the Cumberland Road, James Berry contracted with Hemingway and Company of St. Louis to supply blinds, frames, and cornices for the bridge The material was brought from St. Louis to Vandalia by wagon. Colonel Ross says in his *Souvenir:* "This bridge was undoubtedly the finest structure of its kind in the United States." [4]

Berry is best known in Vandalia for his achievement in painting. It is not known whether he studied under a scholarly artist or whether he was a painter by natural tendency. Nonetheless his talent was recognized by his contemporaries, and Berry's appointment to paint Shadrach Bond's portrait for the new Statehouse in Vandalia testifies to what degree he had arrived in his execution of art. The portrait was placed in the capitol and removed to Springfield in 1839. Vandalians have been under the impression that the Bond portrait was safely kept; however, it can no longer be located. It has been said that grace, facility, taste, and harmony of coloring characterized the portrait as did all the paintings by Berry.

The State of Illinois commissioned Berry to go to the capital at Washington to copy the paintings of General Lafayette and George Washington in the House of Representatives. According to the auditor's reports (1838-1839) Berry was paid $500, in part, for copying the full length portraits, which were to be placed in the legislative halls of the Springfield statehouse. No doubt he received another payment but in what amount is unknown by the author. Berry enjoyed recounting an anecdote about the portraits. The doorkeeper of the House of Representatives, when he proceeded to replace the original portraits in their frames, remarked that he could not distinguish Berry's copies from the originals and asked the artist to tell him. Berry is supposed to have quipped when he returned to Vandalia that he had brought home the originals instead of his own, but no one had discovered the substitution. [5] The full-length portraits by Berry now hang in the Archives Building in Springfield.

In June, 1862, Berry was the only attesting witness to the will of Robert K. McLaughlin at the former state treasurer's death. The other two witnesses to the will were deceased. Berry testified in court that he was present at the execution and signing of the last will and testament in which McLaughlin bequeathed all his property to his wife Isabella. Other than this testimony, little is known of Berry during the last few years of his life except that he made his home with his sister Ann Berry Harrison at Decatur, Illinois. His body was brought for burial to Vandalia. In his will he bequeathed his property to his sisters Ann, Carolyn, and Melinda.

It is unfortunate that so few associations of Berry can be traced. On documents and abstracts his signature appears frequently. Some of his paintings in which his strong personality is communicated to his viewers still exist. For years as circuit clerk he carried on his duties in the old Statehouse when the building served as a county courthouse. His marker can be viewed in the old State Burial Ground. A picturesque spot in Vandalia that has an association with the artist is the quaint Little Brick House acreage, which he owned during capital days. In the cottage is a room devoted to the artist's memory. Although one will not find his name recorded in encyclopedias, James W. Berry occupied a niche that American art can ill afford to leave vacant.

MORRIS BIRKBECK

Morris Birkbeck, the first prose writer of the infant commonwealth of Illinois, was born in Settle, England, January 23, 1764. He perhaps first left his imprint on the thought of the time when he graphically recorded his experiences in a book entitled *Notes on a Journey Through France.* He in company with George Flower of Hertfordshire toured Lyons to the Pyrennees and returned through Toulouse during the summer of 1814 where they studied the habits of the peasants and their agricultural methods—a plan which was quite at variance with the usual sightseer at that time.

In France he saw the benefits of the Revolution upon the land. After Napoleon's defeat at Waterloo in 1815, England frowned upon revolutions or liberal reforms. Birkbeck decided to come to America no doubt because of the unrest due to social conditions. Furthermore, he was a Quaker and men of that belief were restrained from participating in numerous activities, especially those that required joining the Established Church. In America he felt that he would not be hampered by such political disabilities.[6] Although he was a well-to-do farmer with a comfortable home and a prosperous business, he preferred a life of liberty and equal opportunity for all.

It was through Edward Coles that Flower and Birkbeck determined to locate their new English colony in the state of Illinois. During their tour of 1817 they found an uncommonly luxuriant growth of prairie grass in Edwards County where they decided to settle in August, 1818. Morris Birkbeck and his nine adventurers arrived in Richmond, Virginia, in 1818, and then traveled to Pittsburg by stagecoach which broke down on the journey. The group had to walk a distance of twelve miles. From Pittsburg they traveled by horseback to Cincinnati where Mr. Sloo, the registrar of the Shawneetown Land Office, met them and accompanied the group to General Harrison's home in Vincennes, Indiana, where Miss Andrews was married to George Flower.

The group joined the English Colony that had moved into the newly opened land of Edwards County, Illinois. The towns of Wanborough and Albion were laid off in August and in October respectively. Morris Birkbeck with George Flower introduced improved methods of agriculture with importations of fine fleeces and herds of excellent cattle and sheep from England. As president of the first agricultural society of the state, Birkbeck encouraged both the raising of superior cattle and the scientific tilling of the soil. For the transplanting of improvements in agriculture alone Birkbeck is recognized as one of the great benefactors of the state.

When William Faux, author of *Memorable Days in America* (1823), visited Wanborough, he probably bestowed more favorable criticism upon it than other places he saw, for everywhere he grumbled about the lack of hospitality, good manners, and taste. Quite frankly he revealed rowdy behavior, barbarities, and murders to which he gave much emphasis. Indeed Faux himself showed a lack of taste and good manners in reporting his visit to Birkbeck's home, for after accepting hospitality, he spoke frankly of his host and in spots appeared to give offense. The travel account, nevertheless, gives us a glimpse into Birkbeck's life.

Faux, who was a farmer from England, records that Birkbeck received him with a hearty and gracious welcome. But the visitor explains that his host is not always pleased with those who came to see him, and unhappy with his stern manner, the visitors leave the settlement, paying little deference to him. In fact, they are quick to make contentious remarks. Faux describes Birkbeck as a small, erect man of swarthy complexion, happy in his family of four sons and two daughters. Faux stayed several days at Birkbeck's estate of 16,000 acres. He lamented the fact that this comfortable home was built of wood instead of brick or stone, for a fire would probably demolish it. Although the reader senses that Faux was not disposed to appreciate all that was good, Faux does conclude that he had the pleasure of encountering harmony at the home of this "distinguished gentleman."[7]

A description of Birkbeck has also survived in the writings of George Flower, who says that Birkbeck was small and spare in stature but muscular. His frame was strengthened, however, by early labor and horseback exercise, a necessary activity for the supervision of his farm. His countenance was marked by a bronzed complexion due to weather exposure, sharp features, and bright, intelligent eyes. He knew Latin well with a slight knowledge of Greek and a reading facility of French. Flower wrote:

> Mr. Birkbeck was of quick perception and lively conversation, often spiced with pungent remarks and amusing anecdotes. He was a general and rapid reader, and, notwithstanding his business occupations, showed a decided taste for scientific investigation, for which he always found time to indulge.[8]

Although Birkbeck came as a colonist and became prominent as an agriculturist, he received recognition as an early writer of the state. In 1818 a book, published in London, entitled *Notes on a Journey in America* by Morris Birkbeck was offered for sale at the price of six shillings. It was an account of his tour from the coast of Virginia to the territory of Illinois. On his "wearisome journey" he amused himself by keeping a record of events and observations. The book contains an interesting map of the states through which he journeyed. Only two villages Shawneetown and Kaskaskia are marked on the peculiarly outlined map of Illinois.

In the same year Birkbeck published his book *Letters from Illinois*, which was translated into both French and German. It exercised considerable influence in directing emigrants to settle in the state. Birkbeck emphasizes the comforts of frontier life—agreeable and kind neighbors, good food and clothing, music, and books. Wild turkeys, fat and tender, afforded fine roasts for the table. Apples were superior to any other fruit he had seen. Similarly he voices his approval of the new democratic regime: "I love this government; and thus a novel sensation is excited: it is like the development of a new faculty. I am become a patriot in my old age." [9]

On the other hand, Birkbeck does not restrict himself to glowing accounts alone. He speaks of transportation difficulties: "It will be very long before travelling will be pleasant, except in fine weather and on horseback: this is the grand inconvenience of a new country; but it is not to be compared to the inconvenience of living at the mercy of a villainous aristocracy." [10] Furthermore, the administrators of justice in this new country have their trying moments. Indeed lawyers in England would find the situation most unappealing. An anecdote serves the purpose for supporting his point:

> A notorious offender had escaped from confinement, and mounted on a capital horse, paraded the town where the judge resided, with a brace of loaded pistols, calling at the stores and grog-shops, and declaring he would shoot any man who should molest him. The judge hearing it, loaded a pistol, walked deliberately up to the man to apprehend him, and on his making show of resistance shot him immediately. The ball entered the breast and came out behind, but did not prove mortal. He fell, was reconducted to gaol, escaped a second time, and was drowned in crossing the Ohio. [11]

His descriptive passages of Illinois revealing its charm, freshness, and beauty in the fertile stretches of prairie are noteworthy. In response to an assertion that people were dissatisfied and wretched, Birkbeck maintains that the prairies "are as I have described them, rich, beautiful, healthy; and we, who are settled on them are not dissatisfied, or sighing even for Old England; on the contrary, contented ourselves, we are anxious to induce those whom we love best to follow our example." [12] It was no surprise to the readers of *Letters from Illinois* to learn that Birkbeck had declared his intention to become an American citizen. The naturalization of Birkbeck, placed on record April 28, 1819, was the first in Edwards County.

When Governor Coles enlisted his aid in opposing the anti-slavery forces, Birkbeck began immediately to send persuasive articles to the leading newspapers. Readers were impressed by his active mind and energetic writing. Birkbeck's reply to "Americanus" for styling him a "foreign incendiary and exile" reflects his adherence to the dynamic ideals in Jefferson's Declaration, his forcible reasoning, and his effective style. The pro-slavery people were often unscrupulous in their attacks upon Birkbeck. Usually he gave his sentiments publicity through the press under the pseudonym of Jonathan Freeman. In the following communication to the Illinois *Intelligencer*, however, Birkbeck signed his own name:

For the Intelligencer.

To "AMERICANUS", Sir:—Under a fictitious signature you have presumed to stigmatize me, your fellow-citizen with equal standing as yourself as regards this State, with the odious appellation of "foreign incendiary and exile." This you have done to inflame the public mind against my personal character, and to divert it from the arguments I have adduced against the ruinous schemes of your party. It would have been more manly to have attempted, at least, to refute those arguments. You call yourself "Americanus". An American, a true American, declares, in the face of the world, "that all men ar ecreated equal, and endowed with unalienable rights of liberty," and will "pledge his life, his fortune, and his sacred honor," in support of this "self-evident truth." This, sir, is my principle, and these are my pledges; and shall you, who are an advocate for slavery, call me a foreigner?

An exile, too, you are pleased to style me. Unless you chance to be of the few among us who were born in Illinois, you are also an exile from the land of your nativity. Whether this be to either of us a matter of disgrace or otherwise, will depend on the causes of our expatriation. Come forward, sir, in your own name, and state those causes; let us know your standing, with the occasion and circumstances of your removal. I will then do the like; and the public may decide how far you are entitled to reproach *me* as an exile.

You represent me as deficient in due returns for politeness received. In what, sir, have I been wanting on that score, in regard to yourself or any other, to justify the imputation that I am void of gratitude and every virtue? In making a solemn appeal to my fellow-citizens against measures and principles pregnant with calamity, I have performed a duty to my adopted country; and I subscribe my name, that they might judge of my sincerity from the stake I hold, in common with themselves, in the prosperity of the State. You have availed yourself of this, to direct your attacks against my character; thus betraying the weakness of your cause. The falsehood of your statement respecting the proceedings of the conventionalists, has been exposed by others, which relieves me from that task, and yourself from further notice.   M. Birkbeck
WANBOROUGH, Feb. 19, 1824.

Attacks were frequently directed against the character of the individual involved. In 1824 the convention issue became in an increasing degree a cause of disgraceful behavior in Vandalia. The thought that the pro-slavery men were traitors to the liberties on which the United States had been founded apparently did not occur to them. Referring to Birkbeck as a "foreign incendiary," blackguards excited the backwoodsmen to oppose the Britisher. Had not the English people fought with the Indians against them during the war? Too often unscrupulous conduct seemed the ordinary behavior even in the legislature. The intrigues of the lawmakers were more subtle, of course, than those of the general populace who often participated in shameful mobs. On a few occasions even judges were involved in the fracas. A noisy crowd went so far as to intimidate Governor Coles by hurling abusive language at him under the windows of his residence.

When reading Birkbeck's letter to "Americanus," one is able to ascribe to the Britisher the faculty of sound reasoning. He renounced slavery as an evil, having a breadth of view and suitable expression to set forth with earnestness and simple diction what men in Illinois needed to consider. Perhaps at times he wrote passionately, but he felt keenly about the matter; he no doubt expressed what many people felt but could not say. It was actually fortunate that people of Illinois were within the sphere of Birkbeck's personal influence.

Birkbeck's articles were destined to be effective. Too often they received only disapproving attention. But thoughtful people did not regard Birkbeck as dangerous and detrimental. When David Blackwell resigned as secretary of state, Governor Coles offered the position to Birkbeck. On September 22, 1824, the governor wrote from Edwardsville asking him to accept the office: "it affords me pleasure to have it in my power to give you so strong a proof of the high estimation in which I hold your character." [18]

On the night of October 7, Birkbeck arrived in Vandalia. Colonel Field conveyed the news to him that the governor was suffering from illness at his home in Edwardsville. From October 15 until the following January 15, Birkbeck served the best interest of the people with ability and judgment. When he took over the office, he soon restored it to good order where only confusion had prevailed. In the interest of self-government he performed his duties with zeal and good management.

The pro-slavery elements were indeed malicious in their enmity toward Birkbeck and were determined to injure his standing in the state. Although his letter to Governor Coles on February 19, 1824, says, "My private situation screens me in great measure from persecution though I presume, not from the honor of their hatred," [14] he later found that his arguments based on truth and right were so effective that they did not screen him from persecution. The Senate with a majority of pro-slavery men had to pass on the governor's nomination. The injury that would be done to the state was not measured; only the antagonism toward Birkbeck governed the Senate's decision. As a result the Senate refused to confirm the appointment and turned out of office the most capable secretary of state that the infant commonwealth had been priviledged to have. Such an action served to manifest Birkbeck's potent influence in defeating the slavery movement. Birkbeck left Vandalia with a defeated sense of purpose. But he was not forgotten. The Illinois *Intelligencer* carried this item on June 10, 1825:

> By a gentleman who arrived in this place on Wednesday last, we received the painful intelligence of the death of *Morris Birkbeck*, Esq., formerly Secretary of State of Illinois. We understand that himself and son, were at Harmony, Indiana, on a visit, and while there the rains had swollen a small stream called *Fox* river, which was on his route, so much that it was impassable, without swimming. In attempting to swim it, his horse failed and they both went down together!—The son in endeavoring to relieve his father, but without success, narrowly escaped meeting the same fate! The horse was also drowned. In Mr. Birkbeck we have to lament the loss of an intelligent and useful citizen. He was well known to the literary world as the author of Letters of Illinois; which, it is believed have done much towards furnishing foreigners with correct information in relation to the true character of this country.

Nor were Americans alone in finding Birkbeck interesting to read. The fact that Thomas Carlyle alludes to Birkbeck's observations of a society in the backwoods of a new country testifies to his recognition as an early writer. In Carlyle's account of Robert Burns published in the *Edinburgh Review* in 1828, Carlyle quotes from *Notes on a Journey in America.* [15]

Morris Birkbeck has not dropped into oblivion. University students in this area have become acquainted with his writing. Indeed the people of Edwards County have not neglected their eminent citizen. The dedication of a memorial to Morris Birkbeck presented by the Department of Illinois Woman's Relief Corps, Auxiliary to the Grand Army of the Republic, took place at Albion on October 27, 1929. The dedicatory address was given by Governor Louis L. Emmerson. The original English settlement is not alone in remembering its famous founder, for at Vandalia Morris Birkbeck is revered in memory at The Little Brick House (incidentally its architecture is unmistakably English). Both a pencil portrait and his name on the Illinois literary map remind visitors to the old capital that the services to his adopted state have not been forgotten. On display is his book *Letters from Illinois*, an original copy published in 1818. Vandalia is probably one of the very few places in the state where Morris Birkbeck is esteemed for both his writing and his statesmanship.

SIDNEY BREESE

Eminent in the field of law, Sidney Breese left his imprint upon that profession to such a degree that he ranks as one of America's most illustrious jurists. He was born July 15, 1800, into an aristocratic New York family. At the home of Arthur Breese, his father, many distinguished men including General Lafayette were entertained. The young Sidney entered Hamilton College. Later he was graduated from Union College. In 1818 he accepted an invitation from Elias Kent Kane to come to Kaskaskia. There Breese received his admission to the bar in 1820. When Vandalia became the capital, Sidney Breese, assistant secretary of state to his friend Kane, took the state records by ox-cart from Kaskaskia to the new seat of government. He rode horseback while a slave drove the ox-cart. It was necessary for them to cut a path through the dense underbrush and timbered areas at several points. For the service of moving the archives Breese was paid the sum of twenty-five dollars.

Breese served as attorney general and attended court in Fayette County from 1821 to 1824. It was Kane who secured the position for him. On September 4, 1823, Sidney Breese married Eliza Morrison, daughter of William Morrison, a wealthy merchant of Kaskaskia. The child bride was only fourteen years of age; in fact, she was sitting in the garden of her home playing with her dolls when the young lawyer asked her father for her hand. To this union fourteen children were born. Breese was residing with his wife in Kaskaskia when Lafayette visited there in 1825. The Breeses participated in the reception ceremonies honoring the marquis. Eliza Breese was quite proud of the fact that she not only danced with the general but she and Lafayette led the cotillion.

In 1831 the young Breese undertook the publication of a book at the request of the members of the bar. *Reports of Cases at Common Law and in Chancery* included the decisions of the supreme court of Illinois from 1819 to 1831. He addressed the volume to Elias Kane, his early legal instructor. He refers to him as "the oldest practicing lawyer in a country when, when you immigrated to it was an unpeopled waste, now a populous State, and promising fair to become one of the first of the Confederacy." William Wilson, Samuel Lockwood, Theopolis Smith, and Thomas Brown examined the book, finding the cases correctly reported. Included in the book is the case of Edward Coles versus County of Madison in which Coles was released from all penalties incurred under the act of 1819. He had freed his slaves before entering Illinois, but after he had arrived at Edwardsville and had received advice from Daniel P. Cook, an able lawyer, he gave papers of manumission to each former slave. A state law had been passed, however, prohibiting any one from bringing Negro slaves into the state for the purpose of emancipation. The law stated that it was necessary for the owner to give bond that the Negro would not be a county charge. If he failed to do such, he would be obliged to pay the sum of two hundred dollars for each emancipated slave. A suit was instituted against Coles to recover such sum for each slave. The suit has been considered one of the stains on the history of the Illinois judiciary.

For a short period Breese directed his efforts in another field— that of soldiery. When Black Hawk crossed the Mississippi River in 1832 with his some five hundred braves into the Rock River country, Breese answered Governor Reynolds' call for volunteers and served as a lieutenant-colonel. Then in 1835 he was elected judge of the second circuit court. During this time he wrote the opinion in the People versus Field Case in which he held that the governor had power to remove from office a subordinate. Breese has been well known for his sensible opinions relating to the needs of the infant state at this time. Young lawyers can verify that a quotation from Breese is final in the legal profession.

In 1835 Breese moved to a residence on a farm located north of Carlyle, Illinois. Here he and his wife enjoyed social gatherings and entertained graciously the members of the bar. Pieces of Majolica, Staffordshire, and Bohemian glass from the judge's table are family treasurers of his descendants in Carlyle. Even the jet beads that trimmed Eliza Breese's silk and lace dress that came from a fashionable shop in Paris, France, are still cherished. The books from Sidney Breese's library reveal his taste in good literature. The frontier community of Carlyle was not without its individuals who possessed cultural interests and intellectual attainments. Much seems to have been written about anti-cultural aspects of frontier life. Little attention seems to be given to people like Sidney and Eliza Breese.

Judge Breese served in prominent positions throughout his life. In 1841 he was an Illinois supreme justice; in 1842 a United States senator for one term; in 1848 a speaker of the Illinois House of Representatives; and at his death he was serving as a justice of the Supreme Court of Illinois. In 1845 Judge Breese built a new house in the city of Carlyle at the address of 1091 Franklin Street where he and Eliza lived the rest of their lives. The house is still standing in the picturesque town which also has its recognition in history. Carlyle presented its claims for the honor of the capital in 1819 and failed by one vote. It began as a fort on the Kaskaskia River in 1811. Seven years later it was surveyed and laid out in lots. In 1819 a post office was established under the name *Carlisle*, the spelling of which persisted until 1832.

At his death in 1878 Judge Breese was referred to as the "illustrious citizen, jurist, and statesman" of Illinois. An impressive funeral ceremony was witnessed in Carlyle by a large gathering of prominent state officials. Of all his eminent achievements in the legal profession Judge Breese wished to be remembered for his interest and participation in securing the railroad for Illinois. The inscription that appears on his red granite monument in the Carlyle cemetery was his own request made in 1850:

> He who sleeps beneath this stone projected the
> Illinois Central Railroad.

Sidney Breese is remembered primarily for his masterful knowledge of the law. The undertaking to gather reports of cases for an eleven-year period into one volume was a service of no small task to his state. The city of Breese, located west of Carlyle, was named for the successful jurist. Clearly the editor of the *Dictionary of American Biography* refers to Breese's brilliant activity in the courts and in addition asserts: "He was also conspicuous for witty repartee on the bench. His opinions were couched in lucid language."[16] Indeed, Sidney Breese has left his "trail of glory" in the annals of early Illinois history, and it is not likely that his memory will cease to live.[17]

ORVILLE HICKMAN BROWNING

Orville Browning was born in 1806 in Kentucky. At the age of thirty he emigrated from this state, where he had attended Augusta College and studied law, to settle in Quincy, Illinois. In his manners, speech, and dress Browning was a gentleman of the social graces. He very soon became known as a lawyer skilled in using expedient methods.

In 1836 Browning, a conservative Whig, was elected state senator. He became unpopular for a time in Vandalia when he refused to support Lincoln's internal improvement scheme, but in the relocation capital campaign he lent Lincoln assistance. There developed an intimate friendship between the crude backwoodsman and the polished dandy.

In 1836 Browning was married. His wife Eliza, according to oral tradition, was fond of hearing Lincoln tell stories and often would ask him to relate another. He accordingly acquiesced, and during one of those moments she made a crayon drawing of him and called it "Lincoln, the Storyteller." One report has it that the drawing was executed in the Morey building which was destroyed by fire in the 1940's. John Read of Quincy came into possession of the drawing, and for a time it was located in the law office belonging to a descendant of John Reed in Lewiston, Illinois. Where the original drawing is located at the present is unknown. Historians often have much to relate of a gloomy Lincoln, and it is with a feeling of relief that one can turn to a more pleasing record of Lincoln's evenings spent in Vandalia. An entertaining storyteller desirous of making people laugh is the reminiscence of the young legislator that capital descendants have handed down through the years. It is a bit of a shock to them that Lincoln is presented as an unhappy man in Vandalia. But such research is upon substantial grounds—his letters.

Browning served as state senator until 1843. In 1856 he was one of the organizers of the Republican party in Illinois. On the death of United States Senator Stephen A. Douglas in 1861, Browning was appointed by Governor Yates to fill the unexpired term. In the Senate at Washington Browning did not move in the same direction with President Lincoln. He opposed the Emancipation Proclamation and the second Confiscation Act. In 1866 he became secretary of interior under President Johnson by whom he stood loyally. In 1869 he returned to Illinois and became a special attorney for the Chicago, Burlington and Quincy Railroad.

In Vandalia Browning is known for his service on committees investigating the handling of the internal improvement fund. He protested the incompetence of the commissioners who mishandled the state's money. Nationally, he is remembered for the diary which he faithfully kept. It has been historically valuable to biographers of Lincoln. It was Browning, who wrote in his diary upon hearing of Lincoln's assassination: "To my apprehension it is the heaviest calamity that could have befallen the country. But we are in God's hands. His dealings are mysterious—his ways past finding out, but we must trust to his wisdom and goodness". [18]

JOHN HOWARD BRYANT

John, the brother of the poet William Cullen Bryant, was born in Massachusetts in 1807. His father, Dr. Peter Bryant, was fond of poetry and in his library were the works of eminent English poets. On the death of his mother, John emigrated to Illinois, settling in Princeton in 1832. That year his brother William came to Illinois to see him. It was this visit that inspired William to write "The Prairies," a poem in which he gives expression that is both descriptive and reflective. He describes the boundless fields, the golden and flame-like flowers, the graceful deer, the birds, the old oaks, the mounds that overlooked the river, and the "high rank grass that sweeps" the sides of his horse and

—

> With flowers whose glory and whose multitude
> Rival the constellations!

James Hall reprinted only one poem by a distinguished writer of the East. "To the Evening Wind" by William Cullen Bryant appeared in the May issue, 1832. The poem was first published in *The Talisman*, an annual for 1830. John Howard Bryant, who was fond of writing verse, also contributed to Hall's periodical. In his preference for simple stanza forms and interest in nature he resembled his distinguished brother. In the September 1831 issue appeared his poem "A Sketch," which emphasized the pleasure to be derived from viewing the out-of-door world of Illinois. Probably no early writer ever saw the crowfoot, wild geranium, columbine, fern, and lichen quite as John Bryant did. The pleasure of gathering flowers at a "beauteous spot" near a running stream in the forest shade appealed strongly to him as did the peace that one finds there:

> The rippling wave shall pour
>   its quiet voice
> Into thy listening ear; earth's
>   mingled charms
> Shall touch thy soul with
>   magic and heaven's peace
> Shall fill thy gladdened heart.

During the winter of 1836-1837 John Bryant was in Vandalia in the interest of his county. According to Ida M. Tarbell, Bryant attended a banquet at which Lincoln and other politicians were present. Concerning this festive dinner given by a successful candidate for the United States Senate, Bryant says:

> After the company had gotten pretty noisy and mellow from their imbitions of Yellow Seal and "corn juice" Mr. Douglas and General Shields, to the consternation of the host and intense merriment of the guests, climbed up on the table, at one end, encircled each other's waists, and to the tune of a rollicking

song, pirouetted down the whole length of the table, shouting, singing, and kicking dishes, glasses, and everything right and left, helter skelter. For this night of entertainment to his constituents, the successful candidate was presented with a bill, in the morning, for supper, wines, liquors, and damages, which amounted to six hundred dollars.[19]

During Bryant's stay in Vandalia Lincoln came to his room where he enjoyed telling stories and anecdotes about the Whigs' outwitting the Democrats. Although Bryant was not long in Vandalia, it is well to mention in these pages his association with the legislators of the capital. Bryant played a useful role in the development of the infant commonwealth. With his brother Cyrus he began the settlement which is now the city of Princeton. He was versatile in his interests— poet, farmer, builder of roads and bridges, newspaper editor, and brick manufacturer. Primarily he was a farmer by occupation, laboring with great endurance in the course of his work. But as a useful citizen of the community he played a commendable part on the political scene; he is recognized as one of the founders of the Republican party. Although overshadowed by his distinctive brother in literary matters, John Bryant wrote poetry characterized by fervor, fine feeling, and keen relish for the beauties of nature. He has left two books to posterity—*Poems* (1855) and *Life and Poems* (1894).[20] Such is the contribution of John Bryant, brother of America's first poet to be recognized abroad.

PETER CARTWRIGHT

The religious leader Peter Cartwright was born in Amherst County, Virginia, in 1785. His father, a Revolutionary War soldier, fought for the liberties which his son Peter and other frontiersmen enjoyed. When a young man Peter moved from Virginia into the wilderness of Kentucky. Here he became a well-known and popular itinerant preacher in the Methodist Episcopal religion. Certainly his traveling did much to educate him and although he denies that he had time for reading, one cannot accept the fact that he neglected this area of education upon examining his *Autobiography*. His formal education was slight, but Cartwright, nevertheless, was quite a well-informed person.

Vandalia: Wilderness Capital of Lincoln's Land

In 1824 the pioneer clergyman came to Illinois where his circuit consisted of one hundred miles. He moved his wife and family into Sangamon County where he held permanent residence. The rowdy world of Illinois challenged him, and he vigorously used his slogan: "Oh, whip the devil around the stump" as he traveled horseback, crossing large rivers without bridges, making his way through swamps, and eating wild turkey when he was hungry. He was a tough circuit rider, but a fervent one that won many souls to the Methodist religion. Along his circuits his audiences were large. Cartwright's combative spirit, eloquence, and persuasive powers were admired by the backwoodsmen.

The religious leader has almost become a legendary figure in this area; so many humorous tales and unusual accounts exist about him. When a stranger stopped at the Cartwright home one day, he found the children tied to the furniture so that they would not fight while their parents had gone to town. The stranger exacted a promise that they would not fight if he released them. It was the young Peter who retorted, "You try us once." Immediately upon release the children began blackening each other's eyes. Such was the rough childhood of the militant Peter Cartwright. Certainly as a circuit rider in the Middle West he was a fearless fighter if such an occasion presented itself. Compromise was attempted first, but if toughness were in demand to deal with bullies and drunkards, the situation could well be handled by Cartwright. If intruders attempted to break up his camp meetings, he was quick to meet force with force, and he seems to have been uniformly victorious in these encounters.

No doubt Cartwright made numerous trips to Vandalia before he became a legislator. In 1827, along with Governor Edwards, John Reynolds, Edward Coles, Sidney Breese, James Hall, and John Russell, Cartwright helped to organize the first Illinois state historical society. Some meetings were held in Vandalia. In 1828 Cartwright came to Vandalia to take his seat in the House of Representatives. His election brought to public office a man whose ambition was to legislate laws that would aid churches and schools. In 1830 Cartwright served as president of McKendree College's board and for six years served as visiting trustee. Along with others Cartwright was the founder of educational institutions, namely, McKendree, MacMurray, and Illinois Wesleyan.

In 1832 Peter Cartwright defeated Abraham Lincoln for the Illinois Legislature. Cartwright, representing Sangamon County and the Democratic party, introduced bills and worked on educational committees. He believed along with other political personalities who labored in Vandalia that both religion and education made a better civilization in which justice and morality would prevail. He was still a zealous preacher vitally interested in saving souls for Christ as he helped to legislate laws for the state. He felt as Washington that morality and religion are indispensable supports for the success of a democratic nation, and he put forth his efforts to help the people to move in the right direction. He did not enter, however, into the political practices as whole-heartedly as into the religious field.

Cartwright's *Autobiography*, written in 1856, records many vivid and amusing scenes of Illinois, revealing the author's ability as a raconteur. Critics have asserted that it is a self-glorifying account which was "ghost-written." In the preface Cartwright admits that he had little education and no time to read and that he and many of the circuit riders "murdered the king's English almost every lick." Although his style is somewhat clumsy and repetitive, it has a certain force. No better book on the Western frontier gives an account of religious revivals and hecklers at camp meetings. The camp meeting which gave settlers the opportunity to receive religious instructions from a minister was usually held in groves attended by large crowds. At one time when whiskey-drinkers and whiskey sellers threatened to break up the camp meeting, Cartwright asked some officers of the law to help him maintain order. When the rowdies rose against the officers, the fearless preacher entered the fight:

> I then sprang upon him and caught him by the collar, and jerked him over the wagon bed, in which he was standing, among his barrels. He fell on all-fours. I jumped on him, and told him he was my prisoner, and that if he did not surrender I should hurt him. The deputy sheriff of the county, who was with the mob, and a combatant at that, ran up to me and ordered me to let the prisoner go. I told him I should not. He said if I did not he would knock me over. I told him if he struck to make a sure lick, for the next was mine. Our officer then commanded me to take the deputy sheriff, and I did so. He scuffled a little; but finding himself in rather close quarters he surrendered.[21]

Indeed Peter Cartwright will long be remembered as a pioneer preacher with special abilities that enabled him to lead people to accept Christian ways of living. He chose the humble life of an itinerant preacher in order to save souls although his followers gave him little for food and clothing. Such a fiery, dramatic person was one of the truly colorful personalities in early Illinois history.

STEPHEN ARNOLD DOUGLAS

The American statesman Stephen Douglas was born in Brandon, Vermont, in 1813. His father, a young physician, died when Stephen was an infant. Financial circumstances prevented the boy from preparing for Middlebury College. He worked for a time as an apprentice to two cabinet-makers. He then began the study of law in Ontario County, New York. In 1833 he left for Cleveland, resolving to go farther West. The freshness, vitality, and beauty of the Illinois prairies delighted him. He stopped at Jacksonville but found no employment. Ten miles away he learned that a schoolmaster was in demand. He opened a subscription school at Winchester, borrowed books to study law, and opened a law office upon his return to Jacksonville.

At twenty-one Douglas journeyed to Vandalia to lobby as aspirant to the office of state's attorney. Only the governor, lieutenant governor, senators, and representatives filled their offices by the vote of the people. The legislature selected the other public officials. The very short, thick young man was a striking contrast to the tall, slender young Abraham Lincoln, whom he met for the first time. In February, 1835, during the last week of the session Douglas was selected as state's attorney for the first judicial district. Lincoln voted against the promising young lawyer.

On Monday, December 7, 1835, Stephen Douglas was in Vandalia again to attend the Democratic State Convention, the first political one on a state wide basis in Illinois. It met that afternoon in the House of Representatives. There was sharp argument over the good and evil of such a convention. Douglas was one of the organizers in which role he again demonstrated his advanced ideas with a sense of purpose. The Whigs did not move forward with such vigor but waited until 1839 to adopt the convention plan.

As a representative from Morgan County, Douglas came to Vandalia in 1836. The newly elected members were anxious to see this squat young man whose reputation had preceded him. Indeed it was said that the Morgan County schoolteacher had a political wisdom beyond his years. The Statehouse was under construction, but it was not long until the General Assembly met in the new building. Douglas did not hesitate to speak his mind and quite early in the session he figured in several Democratic victories. He celebrated his successes, moreover, by a rollicking time. He was involved in other lively escapades besides the celebration dinner for which the damages amounted to six hundred dollars. The legend handed down by one generation to another purports that Douglas rode a donkey up the Statehouse stairway to the second floor to celebrate a Democratic victory. It is quite possible that Douglas did precisely that for he was very young and equally frivolous and fun-loving.

In spite of this fact, he considered his legislative duties seriously. His favoring a bill for internal improvements in a sensible manner reflected credit on his sound judgment and interest in the state. At this time the abolitionists were becoming strong in their demand to emancipate all slaves in the Union, but Douglas, a believer in popular sovereignty, favored allowing the states to make their own provisions for the slavery question. At only twenty-three Douglas became the leader of Morgan County's delegation and indeed played an important and successful role in the session. He served as the chairman of the committee on petitions. Along with his delegation he favored both capital relocation (it was possible for Jacksonville to be chosen) and internal improvements.

Stephen Douglas entered into the capital festivities wholeheartedly. Douglas and Lincoln did not present a contrast by physical appearance alone. When they were thrown together on a social level, the charming Douglas mastered the situation. The polished manners and handsome face of the Vermonter compared greatly with the crudeness and homely countenance of the Kentuckian. In fact, Douglas is pictured in Vandalia history books as a young man, not as he appeared in his early forties or shortly before his death in 1861.

Indeed, in the capital he was Lincoln's rival who tasted not of defeat. Douglas, an admirer of the fair sex, was a master in the gallantries and the art of pleasing. The wine of his host he accepted graciously, and his brisk talk sparkled. In the candlelighted ballroom Lincoln retreated to the shadows. In the House of Representatives he was the "born" politician whose lead his colleagues followed, but when gliding over the well-waxed floors of the inn with a lady in his arms, Lincoln was most likely trying to determine what means of escape would be the least obstrusive. On a social level, then, Lincoln was overshadowed by his dynamic opponent in the legislature.

A small book was found among Douglas' private papers which contained some autobiographical material dated September 1, 1838, rather hastily written only two years after his service as a legislator. Although the sketch was not written for publication or revised, it shows the style of Douglas:

> In August, 1836, I was elected to the Legislature from the county of Morgan. The contest was a very spirited one, conducted almost solely upon national politics and party grounds.

He continues:

> On the 1st Monday of December, 1836, I resigned my office of states attorney, and took my seat in the Legislature. It was during this session that Illinois embarked in her mammoth system of internal improvements. Before the election I had announced myself in favor of a general system of internal improvements, and was really anxious to see one of reasonable extent and expense adopted; but never for a moment dreampt of anyone's advocating such a wild and extravagant scheme as the one which was finally adopted.

Douglas explains under what circumstances he voted for the bill. His vote was not his own sentiments upon the subject, but he followed the instructions of his constituents. He asserts: "So strong was the current of popular feeling in its favor that it was hazardous for any politician to oppose it." [22]

The young Douglas showed qualities of leadership during the time he served in the Tenth General Assembly. Such leadership continued to be demonstrated when he was a statesman in the nation's capital where he played a crucial role in influencing the destiny of the United States. Allan Nevins, the distinguished historian, writes: "As a parliamentary combatant the most impressive figure in the country was Stephen A. Douglas." [23] Unfortunately, Douglas has been overshadowed by his Vandalia opponent Abraham Lincoln. The real believers of freedom and the right of self-government will never doubt the sincerity, force, and zeal of Stephen Arnold Douglas.

WILLIAM C. GREENUP

William C. Greenup, surveyor of the capital, was born in Ann Arandel County, Maryland, August 28, 1785. Little is known of this enterprising colonizer of early Illinois. Judging from the correspondence which he has left to posterity, the reader would assume he was well-educated. During the first territorial legislature in 1812 in Kaskaskia, Greenup served as the clerk in the House of Representatives, and during the second session of the legislature in 1815, as the enrolling and engrossing clerk of both the Legislative Council and the House of Representatives. He served as secretary at the First Constitutional Convention of 1818 assembled at Kaskaskia. In the constitution a provision was made that Kaskaskia would serve as the capital until the General Assembly directed differently. The convention activities were concluded August 26. A petition was sent to Congress for a grant of land for the new seat of government. Greenup was employed along with Beal Greenup and John McCollum to survey the new capital into town lots.

Greenup was employed by the United States Government to be chief officer and superintendent of the building of the National Road through Illinois. His daughter who married Ferdinand Ernst's son related that when the government sent him gold with which to pay the road laborers, he kept it in a box under his bed. He would then place the gold in his saddle bags and ride horseback to pay the laborers on the route.

In Greenup's letter to Senator Kane November 3, 1830, he refers to a conversation with Judge Hall regarding some political matters including John Reynolds and then he says:

> I have heard from nearly all the contractors on the road and should the season continue favourable during this month, the Timber will nearly if not entirely be removed from the whole route to this place. All appear to be perfectly satisfied,

and will realize moderate profits—I rec.[d] a letter last evening from Genl. Gratiot assuring me of his satisfaction of my proceedings—his letter is very complementary—My estimate for 1831 is app.[d] & will be laid before Congress. I leave here to morrow for Terre Haute along the route to inspect the work. I am sorry I have not funds enough in hand to pay all the contractors; but I presume I shall soon receive drafts for that purpose by the time I return.[24]

On January 16, 1831, he wrote to Senator Kane, I. D. Robinson, and J. Duncan that he had put under contract the "opening and grubbing of the Cumberland Road from the Eastern boundary of the State to Vandalia." He mentions the estimate of funds, the amount of contracts, and the contingent expenses. For 1831 he made an estimate to the Engineer Department, the maximum amount of which was \$87,803.34 and the minimum was \$66,042.50. He explains that the timber has been removed and the central part of the road grubbed from the state line to Vandalia and then warns,

> But without a further appropriation to construct the Bridges and for Grading, the work already done will be of little utility to the Public. The balance of the former appropriation will be insufficient to progress to any considerable extent in making the road useful.[25]

In his discharge of duties as superintendent of the road, Greenup became interested in an area located fifty miles east of Vandalia, where Joseph Barbour had erected an inn for travelers in 1831. Later in 1834 Greenup established, surrounding the Barbour Inn, a town which bears his name. The original part of the inn still stands where the visitor feels he must tread gently on the ancient floorboards so uneven are they that his body seems to be thrusted disturbingly forward or backward. Remodeling and the addition of rooms to several sides of it have changed its early appearance. At present the enlarged inn is operated as the Greenup Hotel. One's imagination is likely to become excited on the subject of adventurious stories associated with the old inn which served those who traveled the prairies. No doubt Cumberland Road travelers pressed forward hoping to arrive before nightfall at the Barbour Inn where safety and a degree of comfort awaited them in this dangerous but interesting region.

A fascinating legend associated with the inn still exists. When the Tom and Sarah Bush Lincoln family and kin came to Illinois in

1830, it is reported that they stopped at this place where the inn was perhaps under construction. At that time some men were building a well of native rock on the northeast corner of the present premises. The twenty-one-year-old lad offered his services as his family encamped under the trees for the night. Although he had spent the day prodding his ox-team, he was willing to lend a hand. The Greenup citizens are happy to show interested travelers the well that Abraham Lincoln is reported to have built. Upon removal of two rocks one is able to see the masonry of the native rock in the well. It is also reported that later when Lincoln served on the circuit he stopped twice at the inn according to his two signatures on the guest registry. [26]

On the lawn of the old Barbour Inn stands a memorial erected in 1915 by the Greenup citizens. Engraved on the monument marking the site of the old inn is the name of W. C. Greenup, who established the town. The land grants, possessed by Greenup property owners, which were signed by William C. Greenup and Joseph Barbour are also means of holding in memory the road superintendent's name.

Additional information about Greenup is further gained by a lecture delivered by W. S. Prentice. The speaker was recalling events when the legislators assembled in the frontier capital. He mentioned Greenup as "a favorite among the young men. Tall, slender, dignified, deliberate, communicative, always in good humor and always smoking—a walking encyclopedia of political knowledge. He knew all the boys, and they all knew and loved him, and he was the political Gamaliel at whose feet we took our first lessons in political economy." [27]

All that remains of Greenup's memory are the brass transit which he used to survey the capital (it is very like the one Lincoln used to lay out Petersburg in 1836), the town which bears his name located on the National Road, and his tombstone in the State Burial Ground. Rarely does one hear of Greenup today except in Vandalia and in the town which bears his name.

Nonetheless Greenup has a singular merit for which his memory should not perish. He not only surveyed the town which is the terminus of the only road actually built at federal expense and under federal supervision, but he was its builder in Illinois. His industry, energy, initiative, and good judgment were largely responsible for its completion to Vandalia. The Cumberland Road, the name Greenup used in speaking of it, might be called a monument to him in Illinois.

ABRAHAM LINCOLN

Elevated by events, independent judgment, and deep thinking, Abraham Lincoln became a commanding figure in the United States. He was born February 12, 1809, in Kentucky. He migrated from his birthplace first to Indiana and then to Illinois where he finally settled in New Salem. Lack of formal education did not hinder his progress. Elected at the age of twenty-five to the state legislature, Lincoln was to serve his first term at which time he would begin to learn the practices that would enable him to become a statesman.

On Saturday evening, November 29, 1834, the stagecoach pulled into Vandalia carrying six legislators from Sangamon County, the newly elected legislator Abraham Lincoln among them. As a novice in the General Assembly, Lincoln took his seat in the House of Representatives and during the session remained rather silent at first listening to the experienced legislators, college-trained lawyers, and self-educated politicians. Lincoln was aware of the training of certain lawmakers whose air, dress, and command of language asserted their scholarly background. He studied their craft with sharp-eyed observation. He noted their firm handling of problems. Here was a favorable environment for him to learn. Lincoln also attended committee meetings, studied bills and measures, and carefully listened, absorbing the knowledge others imparted.

He began to study carefully the rules of the House; he was considering to propose revisions. But he was too inexperienced at this point; as a result, his proposal to revise the House rules was rejected. But Lincoln was beginning to make his mark—to let the other lawmakers know that he was there to take a part in legislative activities. The Sangamon County Whigs, the delegation to which he belonged, were in favor of big schemes. Every county wanted internal improvements. The legislators agreed to provide them which almost ran the width and breadth of the state. Lincoln was busy pushing legislation for transportation improvements. It was apparent that he did not possess a keen judgment for the intricacies of the banking business. Such a scheme posed the problem of selling bonds to raise $12,000,000. Illinois was almost wrecked financially by this wild plan proposed by Lincoln. In his effort to serve the voters of his county, Lincoln was shrewd in maneuvering, if not in government expenditures. In 1835 when a senate bill reached the House requiring the county to bridge the Sangamon, Lincoln was successful in amending the bill for a second bridge. When the Senate refused, Lincoln was quick to remove his amendment and the bill became law.

Since Vandalia had been established as the capital for a twenty-year period, the Sangamon delegation determined to direct their efforts to removing the capital to Springfield. John Todd Stuart, the Sangamon representative who introduced Lincoln to the legal circle of Vandalia, took an active part to reapportion the state so that his county would have increased representation. He reported a resolution for a special session to be held at the capitol in December, 1835. The resolution passed and it gave Sangamon an increase of three members making seven representatives from that county. Such information is interesting in the history of Vandalia, for the seven representatives and two senators had conferred upon them the nickname "Long Nine"—a group of tall men whose total height was fifty-four feet. Before Lincoln joined the group, John Stuart had been considered the leader. Stuart had been defeated in 1836; accordingly, he was not considered a member of the Long Nine. The other six members of the House were John Dawson and Dan Stone, experienced lawmakers; William Elkin, oldest member; Ninian W. Edwards, youngest man (he was only two months younger than Lincoln); Robert Wilson, the least experienced one; and Andrew McCormick, a tall man weighing nearly three hundred pounds. The two senators were Archer Herndon and Job Fletcher. [28]

When Lincoln returned to Vandalia in 1836, the missionary work began! In his climb toward political leadership, he was learning the art of compromise and was performing ably in this new experience. Lincoln and the other members of the Long Nine set about promising a road here and a railroad there in return for support to relocate the capital. Lincoln made every effort to find votes in the legislature to pass a bill removing the capital to Springfield. The bill passed, naming Springfield the future capital, and the Democrats poured forth their verbal thrusts charging "bargain and corruption."

Regardless of the efforts of the Long Nine to remove the capital, in 1836 workmen were busy completing the new Statehouse. Vandalia is not without its legends about Lincoln, the incomparable storyteller. One incident has been handed down from the past with various versions. The legislators carried on their lawmaking as the Statehouse was being completed in 1836. The wet plaster and drafty corridors must have been uncomfortable. Lincoln felt the chill and complained about it to a fellow member whom he met on his way from the Statehouse to his living quarters. "It's no wonder, Mr. Lincoln, that you are so cold, there is so much of you on the ground." Lincoln always enjoyed jokes about himself and good naturedly accepted those about his big feet.

Lincoln was not long in Vandalia until he realized that most of the lawmakers were of Southern blood. The majority who shared the viewpoint that abolitionists were "dangerous meddlers" were from Kentucky and Tennessee originally. To suppress abolition societies was definitely the aim of his fellow members. The Southerners had passed resolutions in the spring of 1836 condemning the printed matter distributed by abolitionists. The legislators in the state endorsed these resolutions, passing by a vote of seventy-seven to six. The victory of the pro-slavery elements by such a substantial margin represented the attitude that still existed despite the fact that Birkbeck's urgent protestations in the press had insured the success of the anti-slavery forces twelve years prior to the resolutions.

When the legislators endorsed the resolutions in which they publicly disapproved of the forming of these societies, the young lawmaker was stirred to action. The legislative body had failed to accept slavery as an evil. Such an endorsement could be viewed as a surrender of the principle which gave the Union its strength. His feeling against the action demanded an entry in the legislative journal. Lincoln, in collaboration with Dan Stone, a graduate of Middlebury College, made that entry in 1837. Twenty-three years later after his nomination for President of the United States, Lincoln proclaimed that this protest still manifested his stand on the slavery issue. The entry shows that Lincoln insisted upon expressing his own convictions although he along with five others was in an isolated position among the lawmakers:

THE PROTEST IN THE ILLINOIS
LEGISLATURE ON SLAVERY
March 3, 1837

The following protest was presented to the House, which was read and ordered to be spread on the journals to wit:

Resolutions upon the subject of domestic slavery having passed both branches of the General Assembly at its present session, the undersigned hereby protest against the passage of same. They believe that the institution of slavery is founded on both injustice and bad policy; but the promulgation of abolition doctrines tends rather to increase than to abate its evils.

They believe that the Congress of the United States has no power, under the Constitution, to interfere with the institution of slavery in the different states. They believe that the Congress of the United States has the power, under the Constitution to abolish slavery in the District of Columbia but that the power ought not to be exercised unless at the request of said District.

The difference between these opinions and those contained in the said resolutions is their reason for entering this protest.

Dan Stone
A. Lincoln
Representatives from the County of Sangamon

In the earlier pages it has been recorded that in March, 1837, Lincoln was enrolled as a practicing attorney in the Supreme Court Room of the Statehouse. During the time that Lincoln served as a legislator in Vandalia, he became a lawyer. On March 24, 1836, Lincoln's name was entered on record of the Sangamon Circuit Court as a person of good moral character. On September 9, 1836, Lincoln was licensed by two justices of the Supreme Court to practice law in all courts of the state. Then on March 1, 1837, his name was entered on the roll of attorneys in the office of the clerk of the Supreme Court. At this time Lincoln was attending the legislature, for he had voted on at least two bills. Although there is no specific record, it could very well be that Lincoln went into the Supreme Court at this time to be enrolled. The fact that Lincoln's name appeared on the list of attorneys means that "he had completed the third and final step then required to be an attorney." [29]

Along with his permission to practice law, Lincoln was also emerging as a speaker of merit. His speech on the state bank issue was delivered in adequate prose, able and convincing. On January 17,

Vandalia: Wilderness Capital of Lincoln's Land

1839, in Lincoln's report concerning the fertility of Illinois soil entitled "Report and Resolutions Introduced in the Illinois Legislature in Relation to the Purchase of Public Lands" he said, "it is conceded everywhere, as we believe, that Illinois surpasses every other spot of equal extent upon the face of the globe, in fertility of soil." His prose even at this time is uncommon in its simple beauty and grace. One letter which Lincoln wrote at Vandalia, regarding a difficulty between Edward D. Baker and William Butler, is characteristic of Lincoln's understanding of men, his tact, and his considerate interest in others. An excerpt from the letter written on February 1, 1839, reflects also Lincoln's directness, clarity, and economy of words:

> There is no necessity for any bad feeling between Baker and yourself. Your first letter to him was written while you were in a state of high excitement, and therefore ought not to have been construed as an emination of deliberate malice. Unfortunately, however, it reached Baker while he was writhing under a severe toothache, and therefore he at that time was incapable of exercising that patience and reflection which the case required. The note he sent you was written while in that state of feeling, and for that reason I think you ought not to pay any serious regard to it. It is always magnanimous to recant whatever we may have said in passion; and when you and Baker shall have done this, I am sure there will no difficulty be left between you.[30]

Lincoln was more concerned about his presence at every voting roll call after the bill had passed selecting Springfield to be the capital. He and the Sangamon Whigs feared that some act to repeal the law relative to the location of the seat of government might be introduced. Indeed General Ewing was still a vigorous champion for Vandalia. Lincoln cast his vote with the majority to pass the bill which incorporated the town of Danville on January 4, 1838.[31] Again with the majority he voted to raise the salaries of the Supreme Court judges to $1,500 a year on February 9, 1839.[32] Furthermore, on the same day he voted on a bill to apprehend horse thieves more effectively and on the passage of a bill to prohibit betting on elections.

From 1836-1839 Lincoln studied the problems of legislation in the Statehouse. He stood firmly on certain issues. He declared that women ought to vote. He was in favor of admitting all whites to the right of suffrage if they paid taxes and bore arms. He served on various committees which often met in the small room between the Senate and the House of Representatives. He was a student as well as a legislator in this Statehouse. Some problems he faced were of formidable dimensions for a man so young. His pursuits at times were impetuous. His scheme for internal improvements was wild and disappointing. Swapping votes to relocate the capital at Springfield was erratic. From his colleagues he often received stern rebuke. But here in Vandalia the chance presented itself for Lincoln to become a political figure of national stature, and he determined to shape his course. Like a hunter he clearly distinguished prints on the ground invisible to others. He not only winced or shook his head despondingly at the injustice of slavery; he asserted himself, defining his position quite clearly. He gave this question his closest inspection and his deepest thinking.

Lincoln had the opportunity to discuss national issues with prominent political leaders who had substantial influence upon his life. Little did he know that later he would be able to cope successfully with the little giant who seemed to exceed him in ability, wisdom, and social graces when he first met Douglas in Vandalia. But later in their political aspirations they were to clash often, and Lincoln was to show his brilliant grasp of the situation. Another leader, Orville Hickman Browning, became Lincoln's confident and adviser during the first year of the Civil War. Edward Baker continued his long friendship with Lincoln in the nation's capital. The spokesman of popular government was seeing democracy growing into a reality. He was moving among men who also believed that freedom and justice must always be identified with America. Ideas that finally blossomed into the cadence and rich thought of the Gettysburg Address were taking shape. Certainly midst the legislative activity Lincoln was an earnest student acquiring knowledge. The Statehouse might be said to have served as Lincoln's law college on the Midwestern prairies; indeed it played a significant part in shaping a statesman who has become a symbol of democracy, freedom, and justice, and at the point of deepest crisis for the nation Lincoln emerged as the savior of the Union.

PIERRE MÉNARD

Pierre Ménard, born in 1767 in Canada, came to Vincennes at the age of nineteen seeking adventure in the West. Employed by

Colonel Vigo' Ménard secured supplies, especially meat, for the army from the Indians. In 1789 he went with Colonel Vigo to see President Washington in regard to the defense of the United States. In 1790 he located at Kaskaskia where he became an active person in the affairs of the community. He served as president of the Legislative Council from 1812-1818 during three territorial legislatures at Kaskaskia.

Ménard did a profitable business in fur trading and became a wealthy merchant. In the spring of 1810 to obtain furs he set out with a group of men for the Three Forks of the Missouri, which was the country of the hostile Blackfeet Indians in southwestern Montana. The Blackfeet carried off their equipment and Ménard returned with some furs. Some of the men departed with him but Andrew Henry and a few remained. [33] Governor Reynolds relates that Ménard was "endowed with a strong, vigorous intellect and was also blessed with an energy that never tired or ceased exertion, only to enjoy rest, so as to be able again for redoubled activity." [34] Popular with both the white and Indian population, Ménard did remarkably well as an agent for the United States in dealing with the Indians who greatly respected his conduct. It has been said that Ménard named the town of Keokuk.

Governor Reynolds comments on Ménard's activities in the state government: "He had a sound, solid judgment and true patriotism to govern his actions in these legislative assemblies. He never made speeches of any length, but like Franklin, told anecdotes that were extremely applicable." [35] He served in Vandalia as the first lieutenant governor of the state. Ménard's private life was equally honorable. Ménard, according to Reynolds was a "liberal and enlightened member of the Catholic Church" [36] and practiced well the doctrines of that faith during his life. His charity to the poor, his kindness to distressed people, and his devotion to his faith were remarkable. When he died in 1844, he was known as a man of great wealth and of spiritual strength.

The memory of Pierre Ménard lives in the county named for him, and in the impressive French colonial home which he erected in 1802. The residence still stands today on a bluff above the Mississippi River, a distance of some fifty miles south of East St. Louis, Illinois.

It is now converted into a museum where one finds many mementoes of the first lieutenant governor. Owned by the state, it is a part of Fort Kaskaskia State Park.

JOHN MASON PECK

A prominent figure in the cultural life of Illinois during the first part of her existence was John Mason Peck, a man of intellectual powers with an enormous capacity for work. His contributions to literature and history are indeed substantial. He was born in Litchfield, Connecticut, in 1789. At the age of twenty he married Sarah Paine to which union ten children were born. In 1813 he was ordained a Baptist minister in the state of New York. During the time that he held pastorates in New York, he developed an interest in Western missions. He studied in Philadelphia to prepare himself to become a missionary, and in 1817 he went to St. Louis. Circumstances were unfavorable to his mission there, and he moved to Rock Spring, Illinois (the name is now O'Fallon).

Here the clergyman rode circuit, traveling tirelessly through the wilderness seeking out families living in the most primitive log cabins. He followed trails which were unmarked in places through dense brush-wood. But the zealous preacher was not deterred. It has been said that Peck traveled on horseback four hundred miles during the month of September, 1818. Bringing into the lives of men and women the Christian religion was uppermost in his mind. This important task made him believe more thoroughly in the system of itinerant preachers, an effective adaptation to frontier conditions. He sought capable men to help preach the Baptist doctrines and employed those who were able to qualify. This direct and practical method of supplying destitute areas Peck felt was an imperative one.

Peck's education brought a degree of enmity among illiterate preachers, and thereby he encountered opposition. Even Peter Cartwright and James Lemen sponsored a bill in the legislature to fine a person who begged money or sold religious literature on the Sabbath Day to support the missions. It was principally the Baptists, Methodists, and Presbyterians who were the strongest denominations in this area. The Lutherans had established themselves in Vandalia at a very early period. At this time Catholic activity was confined to the central and northern portion of Illinois and the French missions along the Mississippi. The Catholic Church did not establish itself in Vandalia until May, 1845, when Father Hamilton celebrated mass in the Senate Chamber of the Statehouse for the first time.

Although actions against Peck were tinged with jealousy, his influence among all denominations in the area was substantial. On the evening of December 8, 1833, Peck gave a lecture on the Burma Mission in Vandalia. Next day the sum of six dollars and fifty cents was handed him by the Presbyterians for the Baptist mission. In fact, Peck came often to Vandalia. He was not only famous as an itinerant preacher, but as an historian he placed great emphasis upon the cultural aspects of history. Early in 1833 Peck gave two lectures, one on Indian history and the other on French history in Illinois, which he delivered in the Statehouse before members of the legislature. [37] James Hall had repeatedly urged the preservation of Illinois history when he lived in Vandalia. He constantly made appeals for participation in historical societies and frequently wrote of past events in his newspaper, annual, and magazine in the hope that people would realize a responsibility toward posterity. Peck and other intellectuals gave their attention to Hall's efforts.

In 1837 another attempt was made to organize a historical society in Vandalia. It was the intention of the members to publish a history of Illinois. Peck was assigned the task of writing it. Such deputation indicates the high regard for Peck's ability. He was to be aided by assistants who would supply information, but the project was never written owing to a lack of financial support. In 1827 Peck was a member of the first historical society under James Hall's presidency. It was Judge Lockwood who served as president in the second effort to preserve the state history in permanent form.

As an educator John Mason Peck made a significant contribution. In 1827 he aided the establishment of Rock Spring Seminary, a school for the training of teachers and ministers. The school was moved to Alton on the Mississippi River northeast of St. Louis. It was renamed Shurtleff College for a Bostonian Benjamin Shurtleff, who contributed $10,000. Until the last few years it continued to operate under that name as a small co-educational college of Baptist denomination offering bachelor's degrees. It is now a part of Southern Illinois University.

As a man of letters Peck has a certain rank. His contributions to periodicals were surprisingly large in output. His numerous articles and reports made him well-known as an authority on the West. At Rock Spring he edited the *Pioneer*, a religious periodical. In 1849 he edited the *Western Watchman*. His editorship of the better gazetteers and emigrant guides were valuable. Peck compiled *A Guide for Emigrants*, which appeared in 1831 and again in 1836 and 1837. Ralph Rusk speaks of the book as "an excellent authority on Illinois and some of the neighboring states."[38] Dan Clark, professor of history at the University of Oregon asserts: "No more graphic summary of the economic evolution of the American frontier has ever been presented than that contained in *A New Guide for Emigrants to the West*, written by J. M. Peck and published in 1837."[39]

Another achievement in which critics find careful first-hand information in a readable form is *A Gazetteer of Illinois* by Peck, published in 1834. It is a small book (6 x 4½ inches) of 376 pages. He writes that the religious denominations at this time are Methodist, Baptist, Presbyterian, Congregational, Cambellite or Reformer, Seceder, Covenanter, United Brethern, Dunkard, Lutheran, Morman, and Catholic. Although his efforts are directed to many subjects, it is interesting to read his comments concerning ministers:

> There is considerable expression of good feeling amongst the different religious denominations, and the members frequently hear the preachers of each other, as there are but few congregations that are supplied every Sabbath. A number of them are men of talents, learning, influence, and unblemished piety. Others have had but few advantages in acquiring either literary or theological information, and yet are good speakers and useful men.
> Some are very illiterate, and make utter confusion of the word of God. Such persons are usually proud, conceited, fanatical, and influenced by a spirit far removed from the meek, docile, benevolent, and charitable spirit of the gospel.[40]

Continuing to be energetic in his writing activities, he wrote a biography of Daniel Boone in 1847 and one of a Baptist clergyman John Clark in 1855. In 1850 he edited a revised edition of James H. Perkins' *Annals of the West*, which had been published in 1846. Peck not only saw his opportunity for participation and leadership in preserving valuable material for the early West, but he had hoped to write a work entitled *Moral Progress of the Great Central Valley of the Western World*. For this project he had accumulated a valuable collection of reports, articles, magazine and newspaper files, sermons, pamphlets, statutes, denominational papers, and much of his own correspondence.

Peck stored his collected material in the old seminary building at Rock Spring. On November 18, 1852, a fire destroyed his library, charring many books and papers, rendering them useless. The event was not totally catastrophic. Some books were thrown out the windows. It was probably the most substantial private library in the Middle West. Indeed many rare collections of newspaper and magazine files were destroyed in the ravages of the fire. [41]

The Baptist pioneer clergyman occupied a leading place in both the religious and civil life of Illinois. The difficult conditions of life on the frontier did not discourage Peck's interest in the continuous moral struggle for each individual. His tremendous energy and ability fortunately were also channeled into useful writing efforts; historians are indebted to Peck for recording important material in the process of the early development of Illinois.

Abraham Lincoln and Other Personalities

ABRAHAM LINCOLN AND OTHER PERSONALITIES

1. G. K. Chesterton, **Come to Think of It** (New York, 1931), p. 218
2. William Baringer, **Lincoln's Vandalia** (New Brunswick, 1949), p. 113
3. Harry C. Blair and Rebecca Tarshis, **Lincoln's Constant Ally** (Portland, 1960), p. 14
4. Ross, **op. cit.**, p. 55
5. **Ibid.**, pp. 44-45
6. Gladys Scott Thomson, **A Pioneer Family** (London, 1953), p. 12
7. Reuben Gold Thwaites, **Early Western Travels** (Cleveland, 1904), pp. 261-268
8. George Flower, **History of the English Settlement in Edwards County, Illinois** (Chicago, 1882), p. 25
9. Morris Birkbeck, **Letters from Illinois** (London, 1818), p. 29
10. **Ibid.**, pp. 27-28
11. **Ibid.**, pp. 61-62
12. Edwin Sparks (ed.), **The English Settlement in Illinois** (Cedar Rapids, 1907), p. 17
13. Alvord, **op. cit.**, p. 159
14. **Ibid.**, p. 151
15. C. L. Hanson, **Representative Poems of Robert Burns with Carlyle's Essay on Burns** (Boston, 1897), p. 4
16. Dumas, Malone (ed.), **Dictionary of American Biography**, III (New York, 1832), p. 16
17. Mrs. Carson Donnell (formerly Euterpe Sharp) by interview and correspondence supplied details of Sidney and Eliza Breese's private life. Mrs. Donnell's mother was reared by Eliza Breese. A few details about Breese's home were supplied by correspondence with residents of that city through Mrs. Donnell's efforts.
18. James G. Randall (ed.), **The Diary of Orville Hickman Browning**, Illinois State Historical Library (Springfield, 1933), p. 20
19. Ida M. Tarbell, **The Life of Abraham Lincoln**, I (New York, 1917), p. 145
20. John Drury, **Old Illinois Houses** (Springfield, 1948), pp. 153-154
21. J. T. Flanagan, **America is West** (Minneapolis, 1945), p. 168
22. Stephen Douglas, "Autobiography," **Journal** Ill. State Hist. Soc., V (Oct. 1912), pp. 340-341
23. Allan Nevins, **The Emergence of Lincoln** (New York, 1950), p. 24
24. Chicago Historical Society, Kane MSS., Vol. LII.
25. **Ibid.**
26. Information secured from Mr. and Mrs. Lee Winnett of Greenup by interview.
27. W. S. Prentice, "Recollections of Vandalia Thirty Years Ago," in **History of Fayette Co.** (Philadelphia, 1878), p. 30
28. Baringer, **op., cit.**, pp. 83-84
29. Information obtained from Dr. Clyde Walton by correspondence.
30. Paul M. Angle, **Abraham Lincoln's Speeches and Letters 1832-1865** (New York, 1957), p. 10
31. Harry E. Pratt, **Lincoln, 1809-1839** (Springfield, 1941), p. 166
32. **Ibid.**, p. 171
33. Dan Clark, **The West in American History** (New York, 1937), pp. 427-428
34. Reynolds, **op. cit.**, p. 291
35. **Ibid.**, p. 293
36. **Ibid.**, p. 294
37. Alvord, **op. cit.**, pp. 323-324
38. Ralph Rusk, **Literature of the Middle Western Frontier**, I (New York, 1925), p. 129
39. Clark, **op. cit.**, p. 306
40. John M. Peck, **A Gazetteer of Illinois** (Jacksonville, 1834), p. 92
41. J. T. Flanagan, "Destruction of an Early Illinois Library," **Journal**, Ill. State Hist. Soc., XLIX, (Winter, 1956), pp. 387-393

PLACES THAT HOUSE HISTORICAL MATERIAL

Here in Vandalia the past lives not because of reconstructed buildings, but because the things that men did in this little town can never be forgotten. It was here that democracy expanded into a permanent idea for our future generations to cherish. It is this fact that makes the past so rich and inspiring, and somehow Americans living in Vandalia become united with the dreams, ideals, and lofty hopes that went into the making of this great country. In Vandalia Abraham Lincoln and Stephen A. Douglas met for the first time. In the Old Statehouse Lincoln protested slavery for the first time as a lawmaker while Douglas upheld popular sovereignty. More than twenty years later their debates attracted national attention. Lincoln, who first developed as a statesman in Vandalia, became president during a war which tested the strength of a democracy. [1]

Joseph C. Burtschi

THE EVANS LIBRARY

Vandalia was host to almost all the early Illinois writers, for they were closely associated with public life. The *Illinois Monthly Magazine* gave the intellectual life of the capital a focus. Hall, particularly, helped to awaken the nation to a sense of its own literary sources in respect to the Western prairies, pioneer types, and native legends. Birkbeck, Cartwright, and Peck familiarized Americans with the West, John Bryant celebrated the woodland scenes in poetry, Reynolds recorded history, and the immortal Lincoln pursued the Jeffersonian frame of mind in political documents. It is indeed appropriate that the first literary center of the state should have such an impressive library building.

The Evans Library houses one of the most significant collections of Lincolniana in the United States. It has been listed as a reference library in the field of historical and social research. The collection, being carefully preserved and guarded against undue handling, is locked in a display case in the Vandalia Historical Society Room and is opened only for reference and by special permission. The general public has access to these materials, and the privilege of handling them is extended to persons who will be careful in the use of them.

The most valuable collection in the library is that of Henry Rankin. In making the gift the donor said, "It is with the thought that it was in Vandalia in the Old State Capitol that Lincoln started his political career." An item that draws much attention is a copy of the cast from the life mask of Abraham Lincoln made by Leonard W. Volk in Chicago in April, 1860. The original mold escaped the Chicago fire which consumed the Volk studio. Fortunately, Volk had taken it to Rome. It is now on exhibit in the Smithsonian Institute at Washington, D. C. The reproduction now on display in the Vandalia Historical Society Room is a cast made from Volk's original. In May, 1915, Herman MacNeil of New York sent to Henry Rankin this copy of the life mask. Near the mask in the display case one reads, "To the artists and sculptors this mask is of indispensable value for with them it has settled forever the bony formation and facial outlines of Mr. Lincoln's remarkable face and head."

Knowledge about the sculpturing of the life mask makes for a greater appreciation when one views it. Lincoln's first meeting with Leonard Volk occurred during the year 1858 when he and Douglas opened their senatorial contest in Chicago. It was the first time Lincoln had ever sat for a sculptor or a painter. He had had daguerrotypes and photographs made prior to 1858. Beside the life mask in the display case is a small thirty-two page book attractively bound with the autograph of the author Henry B. Rankin. An anecdote that lends human interest to the life mask is included in the book. Volk relates that after one of his sittings Lincoln came to his apartment to see his collection of photographs made in Rome and Florence. Volk explained the Grecian and Roman statuary to him and at the same time observed that Lincoln's mind seemed not to be centered on the art. Lincoln finally remarked, "These things must be very interesting to you, Mr. Volk, but the truth is I don't know much of history, and all I do know of it I have learned from the law-books." [2]

Vandalia: Wilderness Capital of Lincoln's Land

Upon further exploration one finds that Mr. Rankin was highly pleased when the United States made provision for a memorial monument honoring Lincoln at Washington, and such a one by the nation presented the same chance for Illinois to mark the events associated with Lincoln in his own state. Vandalia already had its memorial. The Statehouse perpetuates Lincoln's memory in a most fitting manner. Although the massive marble structure in Washington is a magnificent one, it is in one respect a departure from the humility and simplicity which characterized the President. To honor "our most illustrious citizen" Mr. Rankin presented to the library the cast of the life mask.

A rare item in the Rankin Collection is an original photograph of Lincoln, taken in 1857, presented to W. T. Beckman of Petersburg, Illinois. Visitors to the library find this item, which bears a certificate of authenticity, an impressive one. It gives them an opportunity to study closely the unusual qualities in Lincoln's face and to examine the antique oval frame.

Placed with the Rankin items in the display case is a bas-relief of Abraham Lincoln, which was presented by Mrs. Edith West Lameroux. She reported that it had been in the West family since Lincoln's assassination. Being a former resident of Vandalia, she desired the bas-relief to be exhibited in the old capital. Other families of Vandalia have presented items to the library. The daughters of Attorney John A. Bingham, whose interest in the life of Edward Coles led to a publication of an important volume about the notable governor, presented their father's twenty-two books on Lincoln. Volumes on Lincoln from the private libraries of Judge Beverly Henry and Attorney George Houston were given by the latter's widow.

Sometimes on display in the Vandalia Historical Society Room are books pertaining to Vandalia's history. The first one devoted to that subject is the *Historical Souvenir of Vandalia, Illinois*, compiled and edited by Robert W. Ross (1844 or 1843—1928) and published in 1904. The 176-page book (12½ x 9½ inches), covering the history from 1819-1904, contains biographical sketches and accounts of industries, schools, fraternal societies, soldiery, churches, banks, the legal profession, and social clubs. Vandalia citizens contributed their efforts to the undertaking by writing articles about the above subjects.

Places That House Historical Material

The first nineteen pages are devoted to a brief history of the capital period. The book is well illustrated with photographs of individuals, groups of people, residences, and public buildings, particularly the A. P. Field dwelling before it was remodeled, the Divine House of Worship on the site to which it was moved, Governor's Mansion occupied by Bond, Vandalia Hotel as it originally appeared, and the Chartres Tavern. The volume has been of indispensable value to historians and students.

Robert, the third child of Joshua and Martha Ross, natives of Kentucky, was born in Fayette County. He attended the Vandalia public schools and Tuscarora Academy in Philadelphia. Colonel Bob, the name he was affectionately called in Vandalia, was engaged in the drug business and later in the real estate and loan business. The brief biographical sketch under his photograph in the *Historical Souvenir* mentions his political activity—member of the Illinois Legislature, twice chief clerk of the lower house of the Illinois Legislature, and circuit clerk of Fayette County.

The second book that gives attention to the history of the town is entitled *Lincoln's Vandalia* by William E. Baringer. It places, however, more emphasis on Lincoln's early legislative career and the period of his political training with the history of the town serving as a background. The author traces the first twenty-year period of Vandalia from its very beginning to the end of its political importance. There is due emphasis on its buildings; Romaine Proctor's restorative sketches of Chartres Tavern and the House of Divine Worship are distinctive. The five political figures sketched by the artist are equally deserving of attention.

Lincoln's Vandalia, published in 1949, is a small book (8 x 5½ inches) of 141 pages, which represents an inordinate amount of research. The narrative moves directly and effortlessly as the reader feels himself transported into the frontier past. Baringer does not paint a romantic picture of the pioneer capital; neither does he draw an unflattering portrait. Actually the author grasps admirably the significance of the pioneer capital as a subject for social history. It is fortunate for students, historians, and those interested in the early culture of Illinois that Baringer chose Lincoln's political testing ground for a special research subject. He is to be commended for his interest in this fertile field that is too often neglected. The author acknowledges the valuable assistance of the late Harry E. Pratt, distinguished historian and authority on Abraham Lincoln, who gave so generously of his time and talent in helping to assemble information. The book is the first sustained study of the early capital.

The third book devoted to the chronicles of the town is the *Documentary History of Vandalia, Illinois,* edited by Joseph Charles Burtschi. It is a major publication of its kind, according to Harry E. Pratt, who also lent untiring assistance in the assembling of photographs and information for this volume. Primarily written as a gift book, it was presented to the Illinois State Historical Society members attending the autumn meeting at Vandalia in October, 1954. It is different from the Baringer history. As its title suggests, the material is that secured at first hand. The method of presentation is topical rather than chronological. Lincoln does not figure prominently. In fact, all three histories of Vandalia differ substantially in presentation, treatment, and emphasis.

Especially noteworthy in the volume are excerpts from Hall's *Illinois Monthly Magazine* and *Western Souvenir,* Frederick Hollman's *Autobiography* (1819-1827 portion), and travel books by Edmund Flagg, Chester Loomis, and James Stuart. In addition, the book contains illustrations by the St. Louis artist John Matthew Heller, reproduced photographs of political figures and existent buildings, reproduced oil portraits of statesmen, and a few original articles concerning James Hall's literary ventures, the National Road, early transportation, and nomenclature. The major part, however, contains documentary sources.

One distressing point to the editor was that documentation regarding Lincoln's lodging quarters in Vandalia could not be secured. Not even much guesswork exists. He was convinced, however, that Lincoln stayed at the Globe Hotel, operated by Lemuel Lee. The editor replied to the question of its location, "Lee's tavern, which no longer exists, was located on the south side of Gallatin Street down by the river." [3]

An incident relative to the writing of the *Documentary History* lends human interest to the book. When the editor needed advice regarding a research problem or the preparation of his manuscript, he hurriedly communicated the difficulty to Dr. Pratt in Springfield. Later after the publication of the volume, Dr. Pratt smilingly remarked to the editor's daughter, "If I failed one day to receive a telephone call from your father, I felt neglected." [4]

An attractive monograph of thirty-six pages entitled *Lincoln and Vandalia* by Lester O. Schriver and Joseph C. Burtschi, published in 1946, is now a rare item. The narrative, which is both pleasing and instructive, has brought into prominence the Vandalia years (1834-1839)—important ones in Lincoln's development. "Vandalia was the training ground where America's favorite son prepared for stardom in big league politics." [5] The monograph includes distinctive sketches of places, buildings, and paintings. Lester O. Schriver, a graduate of Syracuse University and an attorney by profession, is an author of other monographs and books and a speaker of merit on the subject of Lincoln.

Besides books about Vandalia history and rare items about Lincoln, other reminders of the state's fascinating history are in the display case. A letter from General Ewing at Washington, D. C., to Claibourn Berry, James W.'s brother, marked 1832, discusses Ewing's desire for support in the United States Senate. It is the only letter, written by a statesman who later became a governor at Vandalia, in the possession of the residents of the old capital. A land grant, signed by President John Quincey Adams and dated December 10, 1825, is also in the display case. The Vandalia Historical Society is in possession of a number of documents signed by Governor Joseph Duncan, James Whitlock, and other prominent political figures.

One cherished possession of the Vandalia Historical Society not now on display is a froe which originally belonged to Lincoln. Roy Beck, the great-grandson of Guy Beck, has preserved for posterity the froe which he reports that his great-grandfather and Lincoln used to split blocks of wood. A froe, which is a native term, is a cleaving tool with a handle at right angles to the blade for splitting staves and shingles from a block of wood. Lincoln gave the steel wedge with his initials stamped on it to Guy Beck about 1834. The society members cherish the froe which Roy Beck in his generosity presented to the Vandalia Historical Society as a reminder of the great statesman.

The movement was under way to collect historical items after the organization of the Vandalia Historical Society, founded by Joseph C. Burtschi in 1954.

Before closing a discussion of the Evans Library, it is well to invite attention to its architecture. The building is of contemporary design with no particular style such as the classic. The basic design is due to the site which is long and narrow. Two problems solved by the architects were natural lighting and complete control by one librarian. The obscure glass in the corridor and the clear story above cause the library to be flooded in light. The raising center portion also relieves depression and uninteresting design. The charging desk, workroom, adult and children's sections are all within control of one librarian in order for her to perform her duties in a single area. The space is wide open with no partitions except the entrance corridor, Vandalia Historical Society Room, and sanitary facilities. Screens rather than partitions indicate certain areas. The steel-framed structure (the walls do not support the building) with its curtain walls of masonry, metal accoustical ceiling, aluminum window frames, and concrete floor with vinyl tiles was designed for 30,000 volumes although at present it contains 15,000. The building and the lot cost approximately $110,000.

The library was dedicated Tuesday, December 20, 1960, at which time the donors of the library, Mr. and Mrs. Charles A. Evans, were honored for their munificent gift to the city. The great-grandson of Jeremiah Evans, one of Vandalia's first community-spirited men, has inherited that admirable quality of giving to others. It seems appropriate in these pages to note a few facts for future historians about Charles A. Evans, who was born June 7, 1879, in the 1831 log cabin in which his father, James, was born. In 1888 the family moved to Vandalia where James engaged in the hardware business. From 1904 to 1920 Charles and his brother Albert pursued their father's mercantile occupation. In 1918 Charles turned his attention to a new commercial venture—selling automobiles. He was engaged in that business until 1924. In that year the Springfield Brewery Company, the owner of the Chartres Tavern, demolished the historic inn. An option to build a service station on the site had expired. Charles Evans bought the property and opened in December, 1924, a five story hotel where he accumulated his wealth as owner and manager with a partner. In 1958 Charles Evans sold the hotel.[6] The Evans Library is a monument to Vandalia's philantropist.

THE PRESBYTERIAN CHURCH

As visitors view the Statehouse, another impressive building with sturdy plainess and vitality captures their attention. The structure itself is the oldest church in Vandalia. The Presbyterian Church organization dates back to July 5, 1828. On the site of this old edifice a church was erected by consent of the legislature in 1824 to be used by all religious denominations. Such a legislative act attests to the fact that denominational divisions fade into nothingness when the state interest is involved. It is somewhat surprising to find in this little democracy religious tolerance at a time that prejudices and discriminatory provisions would be anticipated. Such provision for a house of worship clearly shows that the rights of man were assured action by the early legislature.

Furthermore, such an act points to the fact that not all frontiersmen preferred the rough life to spiritual pursuits. A substantial group of people of social distinction found the powerful influence of a church a part of man's life. It is true that another group existed that had a dim perception of the rights of man or the influence of a church. The inns and taverns were focal points for business, political, and social gatherings, but a house for divine worship marked another pattern of living in the social structure of the capital.

The Presbyterian Church, which now stands on the site, was dedicated September 1, 1867, during the pastorship of R. L. Matthews. It was erected at a cost of almost $14,000. In 1953 the members celebrated the one hundred twenty-fifth anniversary of the church. At this time a brief pamphlet containing an interpretative survey of the church was prepared during the pastorship of Roscoe C. Coen, a charter member of the Vandalia Historical Society and an active, vital inspiration to that organization.

The Presbyterian organization is historically associated with James Hall. By December, 1829, James and Mary Posey Hall had professed their Presbyterian faith. Throughout his life, Hall adhered to his faith, being deeply devoted to his Bible and resolute though kind in his Christian actions. He always possessed determination and good judgment to array himself, undeterred by adverse criticism, on the side of justice and morality. His loyalty to the United States and to his friends was manifested during his life, his actions being governed so often by his deeply religious nature.

The Presbyterian Church houses the historical item referred to as the Daniel Boone of Church Bells, the Illinois Riggs Bell, or the First Protestant Church Bell of Illinois. Romulus Riggs, a merchant of Philadelphia, presented to the Presbyterian congregation a bell of fine tonal quality for the cupola of its meeting house in honor of his daughter Illinois. On November 5, 1830, the bell was hung in the House of Divine Worship. Now preserved as a reminder of the early religious influence, it is on display in the main part of the church.

James Hall in the December 1830 issue of the *Illinois Monthly Magazine* wrote an informative article about the first public bell introduced into the state by the American people. The French in Kaskaskia and along the banks of the Mississippi had brought bells into the territory, but the Americans had not brought one to the settlements of Illinois. Hall assigned an illustrious pioneer's name to the bell that "will at some future period, be looked upon as a valuable relic of early times." It was "the very Daniel Boon [sic] of church bells in this region." Boone, revered by his contemporaries as the bold patriot among the great frontiersmen, was held in esteem as the very vanguard of American civilization.

To the people of Vandalia the bell meant ringing out the darkness of ancient practices and ringing in the new era of peace and freedom based on the principles found in the example of Christ. Although Tennyson published his poem "In Memoriam" twenty years after the arrival of the bell, reference has been made frequently to the elegy in speaking of the relic.

At the one hundredth anniversary of the bell Emma Fitzgerald Rice wrote the words "The Old Church Bell" to the tune of "Onward Christian Soldiers." Vandalia's poetry through the years of its life may be to a degree sentimental and inconsequential but it is, nonetheless, sincere, thoughtful, and rhythmical. Mrs. Rice has caught the pulsebeat of the people who treasure the venerable relic:

> May each generation
> Guard our treasure well,
> Hold in veneration,
> And its story tell.
> Then on history's pages
> Men may see its worth,
> Serving through the ages,
> Peace to bring on earth.

At the centennial celebration Norval C. Gochenour said, "While this bell belongs to the Presbyterian congregation, its ownership is much broader than that. It belongs to the citizens of Vandalia; and I think I may voice the hope of this church when I say that future generations will cherish and reverence it more and more as the years roll on."[7] He also said that an important event in the frontier literary world was cause for a centennial celebration, for Hall had published in October, 1830, the first number of the *Illinois Monthly Magazine*.

Joseph C. Burtschi also spoke at the centennial celebration at which time he said, "Take us back, Father Time, in spirit to the day when the voice of this bell was first heard filling the air far and near, reverberating over the hills and through the valleys with prolonged and multiplied effect."[8] It is not the peal of the bell that has spread its influence; today it performs a service that is not in the function of a bell. It silently invites attention to history's pages:

> I have been cared for fondly by the Presbyterians, and I wish to remain in the tranquil beauty of this temple, but "the larger heart, the kindlier hand" will know that I belong to all denominations in Vandalia. May the people live in that spirit of religious tolerance to show others that our American principles, Christlike in their inception, are practical. I am not sectarian. I am American.

In Vandalia a certain segment of society is adhering to the essentially American principle of religious tolerance. When the Vandalia Historical Society met in September, 1955, in the basement of this Presbyterian Church, its pastor was host to the society which has a preponderance of Methodists in membership. A Catholic priest presented the memorial tribute for a deceased member who had practiced the Lutheran religion. It is quite possible that the Baptist pastor delivered the invocation and benediction; he said the prayers on so many occasions for the society. It is noteworthy that on the site of the House of Divine Worship, religious tolerance is still practiced as it was almost a century and a half ago.

THE LITTLE BRICK HOUSE

THE LITTLE BRICK HOUSE

Travelers viewing historic spots of Vandalia often inquire about the pioneer houses. A quaint and picturesque dwelling, similar to those erected during capital days, is the century-old Little Brick House. The property is connected historically with three Vandalia citizens—Charles Prentice, James W. Berry, and Joseph C. Burtschi. Prentice was Vandalia's first store-keeper who owned the property for a short time while Berry owned it for a longer period of time during capital days. Joseph C. Burtschi lived in the house during the earlier part of the nineteenth century.

In 1957 the dwelling with its trim architecture, quaint garden, fine shaded lawn, and brick pathways was restored to its former beauty. The prevailing type of architecture during capital days was modified Georgian with classic arrangement of windows and door, characterized by a note of simplicity and freedom of ornamentation. The white brick house with its red wooden-shuttered windows, plain in plan and in appearance, has simple lines. The windows are proportionately spaced with slit shutters; the small pillared porch was a later addition. It was originally a five-room dwelling with two rooms upstairs and three on the ground floor facing south to take advantage of the sun. Judging by actual sketches and photographs, one can reasonably assume that the Little Brick House recaptures the style of that era.

Soon after its purchase in 1956 the Little Brick House rose triumphantly from the assaults of past years although it needed only a modicum of reconstruction. Most of the original effects were there at its purchase except the fireplace which had been removed from the room adjoining the old parlor. Partitions, windows, doorsteps, wood panelling, the cistern pump, box locks, and porcelain hardware on the windows were kept. The solid walnut balustrade was restored to its former richness and beauty when the varnish was removed. The balusters upon close examination were found to be somewhat uneven in width, indicating that they were fashioned by hand. The shutters were in remarkably good condition; only a few slats were supplied by a carpenter. Paper of documentary design was placed on the walls, and paint to blend with it was applied to the woodwork and interior doors.

Certainly the residence is well framed with trees and plantings. Three magnificent Norway maples that shadow the front lawn attest to the fact that not all the hardwood forest population has dwindled to reduced size. A handsome water oak on the adjoining property is estimated to be over two hundred years old. A graceful walnut tree stands poised and symmetrical in the garden at the rear. Unfortunately, the great walnut population has been almost depleted in Vandalia where once stood these rugged native trees. A wild black cherry and a red mulberry, both native trees, grow side by side near the west parlor window. Shapely Norway maples abound in various sizes on the lawn.

Flowering shrubs that flaunted their beauty during capital days are interesting to the visitor. Early Western writers mention the lilac, flowering almond, and althea (it is commonly called the Rose of Sharon) as the shrubs that flourished. The lilac ranging from shades of lavender to deep blue blooms in early May. The little pink buttons of the flowering almond make their showy appearance somewhat later. In midsummer the althea producing white, pink, lavender, and violet flowers when other shrubs have had their blooming period is an attractive bush on Midwestern lawns.

Vandalia: Wilderness Capital of Lincoln's Land

The brick pathway leading to the front door lends an early day atmosphere to the property. A very narrow entrance hall and a modest stairwell are found at the front entrance. With heating facilities limited to fireplaces and wood-burning stoves, a compact house was suitable to economy, and certainly compactness seems to be a special feature of the entire plan of the construction. At the left the visitor enters the Prentice Room, which affords him a view of furniture owned by pioneer families of the area. The pieces throughout the dwelling are primarily walnut with some oak, maple, mahogany, poplar, and pine. Most of them are simple but tastefully designed. In early days furniture was sturdy and unpretentious, usually taking the form which was easiest to make and most practical to use.

It seems appropriate at this point to record a conversation that occurred in this room. The Little Brick House is not without its anecdotes. The Swiss bell tinkled one morning to announce a visitor. The hostess on duty hurried to welcome the guest but instead found a postman stacking packages on a chair. "Does Abraham Lincoln live here?" he asked.

The present tense escaped her. Visitors often ask the question Did Lincoln live here? "He didn't live here," she answered graciously, "but he may have been on this property at some time."

"Look," he said as he handed her a small package from the United States Printing Office. It bore the address,

> Abraham Lincoln
> 621 St. Clair Street
> Vandalia, Illinois

At first she was puzzled. Suddenly her expression brightened. "Oh, now I can tell visitors that Lincoln's mail was addressed to this house." [9]

The Berry-Hall Room adjoins the parlor with the same kind of tall windows ($6\frac{1}{2}$ x $2\frac{1}{3}$ feet), set with old fashioned panes of glass, some cracks across them. The mahogany sewing table, maple rocker, and walnut day bed, primitive walnut desk constructed with wooden pegs, oak chest of drawers, and walnut tabouret with inlay design are somewhat rare items in the area. The restored fireplace in the north wall derives its beauty from a simple design of pink and blue tiles which originally came from two old dwellings. With its folk art, pencil portraits of capital-day figures, and original Lincoln photographs, the room gives tribute to Vandalia's most notable artist, James W. Berry, as well as Vandalia's first writer, James Hall.

Places That House Historical Material

Upon the walls, maps and pictures recall to mind the history of Illinois. A literary map of the state includes names of approximately one hundred and thirty authors and art sketches relative to subjects used by the writers. Pencil portraits of Stephen Douglas, Morris Birkbeck, James Hall, and Mike Fink form an interesting group on the wall. Two likenesses of the dynamic keelboatman are displayed since it was in Vandalia that Fink bowed into American fiction. In the early nineteenth century as cargoes of corn, oats, and wheat were sent down the Ohio River, the boatmen who pushed long poles against the current were a tough group. The river valley echoed with the shouting of spirited boastfulness of these men. The most fearless braggart was Mike Fink, who was a great shot and a vigorous fighter. Today probably the most famous folklore tales of the Middle West are those of Mike Fink. The other likeness of the boatman appears on a colorful folk-art map (28 x 22 inches) of Vandalia. Political figures, original buildings, Pete Featherton, and reminders of the past such as Kickapoo Indians, buffalo, and covered wagons are included. The pictorial map of Vandalia serves to remind Americans of their historic past.

The dining room which adjoins the Berry-Hall Room offers the visitor a view of a linen press, dropleaf table, chest of drawers with carved wooden drawer pulls in the fruit motif, and a handbevelled mirror. Two maple chairs of 1840 vintage, the seats of which have recently been caned, and a square inlaid table of decorative design are the only non-walnut pieces. On the top of the inlaid table many minute pieces of walnut, cherry, oak, pine, maple, gum, and cedar are inserted in geometric design. Six new walnut slat-backs, bottomed in split white oak, are reproductions of chairs used in the pioneer home.

A frame kitchen was added in the latter part of the nineteenth century. The dado, a wood paneling, is retained. The pitcher pump with bright brass adds a decorative touch as do the walnut shelves on the walls and above the doors. The economic status of the early settlers is recorded in the simplicity of all equipment. Lining the walls are treenware, china, cooking utensils, earthen ware, and flat irons. The side bow chairs are different in size, wood, and design. The china canister set, lettered in German, adds a bit of color and distinction to the otherwise simply furnished kitchen.

Distinctive of the Little Brick House are the gardens which have a special concern for Americans interested in pioneer living and natural beauty. Outside the kitchen door stands a rain barrel which when full contains approximately thirty gallons of water. Rain water caught in this manner was used by the early settlers. A brick walk leads to a well. Almost every pioneer family sank a shaft into the earth to obtain a supply of drinking water. James Hall maintains that there was no dearth of water although the traveler, not finding water upon the surface, reported its absence in this region. Hall explains that there were few spots where water could not be obtained by digging the depth of eighteen to twenty-five feet, and the performance of sinking a well was comparatively easy and successful. [10]

Another brick pathway leads to the outbuildings—the original summer kitchen and woodshed. Nearby is a wooded grove where violets, buttercups, columbines, trilliums, wild blue phlox, and bluebells bloom in the spring. Violets grow so abundantly they cover almost the entire garden. The fruit trees predominantly cherry, apricot, plum, and peach and the kitchen-produce area very pointedly bring to the visitor's mind that each pioneer family possessed an orchard and a garden. Probably no other home in Vandalia meets so well James Hall's description of the earlier villages in this area: "Gardens stocked with fruit trees and flowering shrubs, encompassed the dwellings."

A bird watcher will especially enjoy the gardens. In winter he may hear the clear, vigorous song of the titmouse or see a downy woodpecker running up and down the tree trunks probing the bark for insects or note the chickadees lunching from the bird feeders. The slate-colored junco, winter wren, purple finch, and red-bellied woodpecker along with the year-round residents, cardinals and blue jays, might be seen eating at the food trays or winging their way through the trees. In spring and summer robins, catbirds, flickers, red-throated humming-birds, mourning doves, goldfinches, house wrens, Baltimore orioles, and brown thrashers abound. No bird or flower in the area cheapens the array of the cardinal that reigns supreme in the gardens as it does in the whole wood-world of Illinois.

Places That House Historical Material

The Little Brick House serves a meaningful purpose—to shed light upon the story of an old town and the manner of pioneer living. It is fortunate that visitors to the old capital have an opportunity to see the preservation of this state's architectural, cultural, and social heritage and the protection of a landscape concerned with the early natural beauty of Illinois.

PLACES THAT HOUSE HISTORICAL MATERIAL

1. The paragraph, written by Joseph Burtschi at the age of eighty-six, is the last material which he wrote concerning Vandalia history.
2. Henry B. Rankin, **Our First American Abraham Lincoln** and **The Lincoln Life-Mask** (Springfield, 1913), p. 14
3. Burtschi, **op. cit.**, p. 79
4. The comment was made to the author in the Hotel Evans Dining Room.
5. L. O. Schriver and J. C. Burtschi, **Lincoln and Vandalia** (Peoria, 1946), p. 4
6. Information obtained from C. A. Evans by interview.
7. The Vandalia **Leader**, Nov. 13, 1930
8. **Ibid.**, Nov. 13, 1930
9. The author was present during the conversation between Josephine Burtschi and the postman.
10. James Hall, **Statistics of the West** (Cincinnati, 1836), p. 106

JAMES HALL AND LITERARY ACTIVITY

James Hall, the foremost literary pioneer of the early West, was born in Philadelphia, August 19, 1793. Both his parents, John and Sarah Ewing Hall, were descendants of British families. His paternal ancestors had established themselves in the United States at the end of the seventeenth century while the Ewings came to America early in the eighteenth century. Being a delicate child, James studied at home under supervision. When he entered a Philadelphia academy later, his independent spirit and hatred of illogical discipline prevented him from adjusting to academic surroundings. The fondness for reading which he early acquired in life was not hampered, however, by his formal education. [1]

His study of the law was interrupted by service in the War of 1812. At the end of the war he applied for an army post. As an artillery officer he accompanied Stephen Decatur to Algiers. From August 6 to September 11, 1815, Hall kept a diary which contained colorful events recorded by a writer of acute observation. He resigned from the service in 1818.

In that year he went to Pittsburg where he drifted for a short period and then resumed the study of law. After his admission to the bar he practiced very little in the profession but turned to the unexplored wilderness of the West. In 1820 he boarded a keelboat down the Ohio and landed at Shawneetown, Illinois, where he began the practice of law. It was not long until Hall was editing the Illinois *Gazette*. On his way down the Ohio he had written a series of letters which his brother Harrison Hall, publisher of the *Port Folio*, printed in his periodical from July 1821-May 1822. The *Port Folio* (1801-1827) was the first noteworthy literary magazine in America; it enjoyed wide-spread favor superior to that of all earlier periodicals. Some of the letters Hall had previously published in the *Gazette*.

His marriage to Mary Harrison Posey, who was a granddaughter of General Thomas Posey, a Revolutionary War soldier, took place in 1823. Hall was attaining success in his law practice and prominence as a speaker. As prosecuting attorney he won the first murder trial in the state. When Lafayette came to Illinois in 1825, Hall had the honor of delivering the address of welcome at Shawneetown. It was during the years 1825-1827 as circuit judge that Hall had the opportunity to observe the life of the backwoodsmen in Illinois.

In 1827 the Illinois Legislature appointed James Hall state treasurer, the position which brought him to the capital. Here he lost little time in directing intellectual activities. He was instrumental in the formation of a state historical society. In December, 1827, a group of citizens met in the Statehouse for the purpose of organizing a society devoted to the study of Illinois history. James Hall was elected president with ex-Governor Coles acting as vice-president along with William Wilson, chief justice of the Supreme Court. James Whitlock was elected secretary and R. H. Peebles was named librarian. At these meetings and at Fourth of July celebrations in Vandalia, Hall made speeches that received praise for the thought as well as the precise phrasing. When James Stuart, author of *Three Years in North America*, visited Vandalia in the spring of 1830, he had high praise for the published proceedings of the society. He mentioned that the organization was so well conducted that its seat might have been at Cambridge or Oxford. Unfortunately, the Antiquarian and Historical Society of Illinois had a brief existence, for when Hall departed from Vandalia, it was not long until the society ceased its activities.

Very few pioneer towns could boast of a resident whose book had been published in London. In 1828 *Letters from the West* by James Hall appeared, and from it readers were learning of the scenery, manners, and customs of the West. These were the letters, with additions, that had previously been published in the Illinois *Gazette* and the *Port Folio*. Unhappily, the editor of the *Quarterly Review* of London ridiculed the book. He resented Hall's anti-British attacks, but Hall, on the other hand, could not allow misrepresentations of America found in English periodicals to go unnoticed. Merle Curti, a twentieth century critic, refers to the book as "a remarkable account of the geography, people, manners, and life of the frontier country."[2] At the time of publication readers on both sides of the Atlantic, despite the British attack, found *Letters from the West* a delightful and refreshing travel book.

THE WESTERN SOUVENIR

Hall continued to have the keenest zeal for producing literature that would assume a role in the development of American culture. In 1828 he conceived the idea of editing an annual or gift book for the Christmas season. At this time there was a vogue in favor of these little books which contained tales, poems, and articles. A number of annuals had appeared in the East and abroad to such an extent that it became quite fashionable to have one adorning the parlor table. Hall entitled his annual *The Western Souvenir for 1829, a Christmas and New Year's Gift* and bound it in heavy, bright red silk. Contemporary critics were somewhat unfavorable. Later in Ralph Rusk's important survey of Middlewestern literature a reference is made to Hall's book as "the first important challenge of this kind" that represented the West among the annuals.

The small book (3 x 5½ inches) of 324 pages included the type of material found in other gift books. Hall contributed approximately one third of the contents which were rich in regional scenes and characters. Timothy Flint's "Oolemba in Cincinnati," a tale of a Delaware warrior, and two poems entitled "The Minstrel's Home" and "The Stranger's Grave" by Otway Curry were included in the contents.

The most prominent item in the book was Morgan Neville's story "The Last of the Boatmen." This story is notable, for it marked the first appearance of the legendary king of the keelboatmen, Mike Fink. Not too long after Fink's introduction into literature, his prowess with his fists, his precise marksmanship, and his fabulous skill as a keelboatman became mythical recountings. Actually he was a real person, but his skill at handling a keelboat paddle and an adversary in a fight has become exaggerted to such a degree that Mike Fink is now a part of Midwestern river lore. Writers since have found this one-time terror of the Ohio and Mississippi a fascinating subject for legend material.

What appeared in Neville's story, when one judges it by standards of modern writing, is a rather proper account, excluding the river brawls and other seamy experiences associated with the fabulous folk-hero. Neville relates a rather seemly feat of Fink's shooting off a tin cup placed on the head of his brother who stood thirty yards from him. The fame of Fink has grown fabulously since this first story. Indeed the "gigantic form of Mike, bestriding the large steering oar" has become Gargantuan in proportions, and certainly the legends of this keelboat king are an example of how stories grow taller.

"Pete Featherton," "The Indian Hater," and "The French Village," three of James Hall's well-known stories, were included in the *Western Souvenir.* "Pete Featherton," it appears, is the critics' favorite. Van Wyck Brooks believes it to be Hall's best. John T. Flanagan maintains that it is one of the best early American tales. Rufus Griswold in his volume, a brief survey of intellectual history concerning the writers who had a motive force in controlling the national mind, includes "Pete Featherton" as the story representing Hall's best.

The very beginning of the tale has an amusing tone that continues to the end. Hall maintains that imaginary beings such as ghosts, brownies, and witches have not emigrated to the new country. In fact, the frontier had no accommodations for them—no baronial castles, ruined mansions, or ancient abbeys for them to inhabit. Pete Featherton wore his usual hunting clothes as he set off to pursue the deer. "His feet were cased in moccasins, and his legs in wrappers of dressed deerskin" and "accoutered with a powder-horn, quaintly carved all over with curious devices,—an ample pouch with flints, patches, balls, and other 'fixens.'" The reader's interest is captured at the onset and fails to waver as he travels with the bold, young backwoodsman who sallies forth with his rifle "Brown Bess" on his shoulder and with an ax chops a path through the wilderness. Pete's meeting with the gray-bearded, thin old man who blew his breath upon the rifle and charmed it, the breaking of the magic spell, the Indian doctor's instructions, and Pete's gun restored to favor are all a part of the folklore and superstition that Hall uses in his tale. Certainly he manages the storytelling quite competently, bringing the enchanted rifle legend to prominence with other folk tales that have grown so colorful with the years.

In "The Indian Hater," as the title suggests, Hall relates the story of one settler's bitter hatred for the redskins. Although Hall usually saw the better side of the Indian character, he based this story on an account which involved a savage tribe. During the course of a journey through Illinois, Hall's attention was drawn to Samuel Monson, whose keen, grim, and resigned expression puzzled him. At the presence of several Indians who entered the store at which place Hall observed this man, Monson started to grasp his knife and at the same time his face changed to a vehement expression. When the Indians departed, Monson started to follow them but the men present in the store withheld him.

The suspenseful story moves swiftly. Hall does not learn the reason for Monson's intense hatred until Hall's Pottowattomie guide is suddenly killed by ambush. It was Samuel Monson who emerged from the bushes. Hurriedly he proceeded to tell Hall that his entire family had perished in the flames of his cabin which Indians had set on fire. The desire for revenge had so gnawed at Monson's heart that he promised to kill every redskin whom he would meet.

The dramatic force and direct narration are strong qualities, but Hall's use of rich local color is also a dominant feature of "The Indian Hater." Graphically and gracefully Hall describes the prairies: "The whole is overspread with grass and flowers, constituting a rich and varied carpet, in which a ground of lively green is ornamented with a profusion of the gaudiest hues. Deep recesses in the edge of the timber, resemble the bays and inlets of a lake; which occasionally a long vista, opening far back into the forest, suffers the eye to roam off and refresh itself with the calm beauty of a distant perspective."[3]

"The French Village" is the story of a small, hospitable community near the banks of the Mississippi. *Charivary*, the custom of serenading at the marriage of a widow or widower, still prevailed among the French inhabitants. Some of the new settlers, not understanding the ancient custom, proceeded to have a *charivary* at the marriage of Jeanette Duval and Baptiste Menou. Since neither had been previously married, Baptiste was bewildered when he heard the flutes, fiddles, cow-horns, kettles, and drums. He accepted the serenade with good humor, however, and invited the merry villagers into his house. An old Frenchman who found it disgraceful to have a *charivary* for a maid and a bachelor blamed the new American government that was beginning to occupy French land on the Mississippi. He sputtered: "Dis come for have d'American government to rule de countrie. Parbleu! they make charivary for de old maid and de old bachelor." [4] Hall admirably captured the dialect of these inhabitants throughout the story.

Readers do not often discover how sharp is Hall's satire which is obviously the intent in this story. Perhaps his genial humor has carefully cloaked his philosophical intent to such a degree that it escapes the reader's attention: "——they enjoyed to the full extent, those three blessings on which our declaration of independence has laid so much stress—life, liberty, and the pursuit of happiness." [5] When the jurisdiction of American government extended to this region, justices of the peace, constables, and sheriffs were dispersed. The good French shook their heads for certainly the new settlers intended to be wicked. But when the newcomers went to the length of enrolling them in the militia, this was no longer the country for them. With the Yankee emigration the happy, freedom-loving villagers moved elsewhere. But Jeanette and Baptiste remained on the soil of their fathers and alone carried on the traditions where the village of happy, congenial French no longer existed, and the story ends on a note of sadness.

The poetry included in the *Western Souvenir* shows a fluency and ease, but it is not distinguished verse. Hall's talent for humor is found in the gay, little poem, a parody of Scott's "Lochinvar," entitled "The New Souvenir," which serves to introduce the annual to its readers:

> One hand to the paper, one touch to the pen,
> We have rallied around us the best of our men:—
> Away with the moccasin, rifle, and brand!
> We have song, picture, silk, and gold leaf
>   at command— [6]

A poem to a Shawnee warrior, a member of the most hostile Indian tribe of Illinois, is one that Hall wrote when he lived at Shawneetown. He submitted it for publication in 1822 to the *Port Folio*, which printed it under the title "Lines Written on the Banks of the Wabash." In the annual it appeared under the title "The Shawanoe Warrior." Although it lacks a sharpness of image and detail, it has a pleasing rhythm. Hall handles the anapestic trimeter skillfully:

Wher'er in the dark winding dell.
Or the prairie, in ambush he lay,
The huge elk and buffaloe fell,
And the nimble wild deer was his prey.
But in war was the chieftan's delight;
No warrior more valiant than he,
There was none in the bloodiest fight,
More fierce than the bold Shawanoe.[7]

Another poem in which Hall utilizes the aborigine is "The Forest Chief," a ballad of twenty-eight stanzas. In spite of flaws of construction "The Forest Chief" reaches a certain pitch of emotional intensity. The poem can hardly be regarded as successful artistically speaking, but indeed it is one in which Hall portrays the individual redskin as a human being rather than a ferocious savage on the frontier. It is the story of a painted warrior who appears before grief-stricken parents, lamenting the loss of their child to the Indians. The chief promises recovery of the child or death to the prowling Muskogee who holds the boy captive. The warrior returns with the boy, the parents clasp their child to them, and then turn to thank the Indian who has already vanished from sight.

The striking musical quality of Hall's verse is seen in his lyric "A Gift," in which he expresses himself in trochaic meter. The poem first appeared in the *Western Souvenir*. It was reprinted over a century later in a gift book edited by Joseph C. Burtschi. The historian was offering a gift to the state society members that he hoped would be "treasured long and dear" and such was "friendship's offering." The words by James Hall expressed the precise sentiment of the historian. [8]

Part of the special value of the *Western Souvenir* is in its pictorial art. The decorative figures and narrative illustrations that augment the text were contributed by artists noteworthy in their field. Steel-engravings which pictured scenes of mountains and rivers were in their heyday. Illustrators and painters found that the American scene had its own particular charm. In the *Western Souvenir*, however, the illustrations depicting mountains with masses of rock were actually a misrepresentation of the prairie scene.

On the title page appears Henry Inman's drawing of a dark-haired young woman holding a wreath in her hand and resting her arm on what appears to be a sizable rock. Inman, who was the major art contributor for the *Talisman*, an Eastern annual, was considered the most patronized portrait painter in New York at the publication of Hall's gift book. It was Henry Inman who painted the portrait which "Mrs. Wordsworth considered the best that had ever been made of her husband"[9] when Henry Reed arranged an American edition of the nature poet's work. Inman also executed genre paintings in America. When Hall in collaboration with Thomas McKenny published *The Indian Tribes of North America*, that notable achievement, Inman painted the Indian portraits and scenes.

Other embellishments are the Shawanoe Warrior, a view of Frankfort, and one of Cincinnati by Samuel M. Lee. *The Peasant Girl* by August Hervieu precedes the story "The French Village." George Lehman executed the view of Pittsburgh. Edward William Clay, an etcher and engraver of Philadelphia, also furnished a drawing. Today few of his etchings or other work survive according to the editors of the *Dictionary of American Biography:* "Clay was an artist who had a fresh, original manner and a fancy that was not bound by convention; his only fault was that he made far too few drawings."[10] Edward Clay's illustration, *The Deserted Children, an Island Scene of the Ohio*, depicting three frightened youngsters as several Indians approach them, appears opposite Hall's true incident entitled "The Deserted Children." The happening concerns three children whom the father left on an island in the Ohio upon his departure to a nearby place. The father became intoxicated after joining in conversation with a group of men. He was drowned attempting to return to the island. In the meantime several Indians came to the island and built a campfire. The eight-year-old, the eldest child, fearlessly led the young ones to the campfire where the Indians treated them kindly, even conducting them to the nearest town where white settlers cared for them.

Perhaps the chief distinction of the *Western Souvenir* is that it was the first annual published on the Western frontier. Excerpts of an address by Benjamin Drake, delivered before the Erodelphian Society of Miami University, were recorded in the January 1832 issue of the *Illinois Monthly Magazine:* "Are there no more Mike Finks on our rivers? no more Pete Feathertons in our woods?—Are the Indian traditions all told, and the border legends all sung?" It was fortunate such legends were told at all. Writing in which Western material was utilized in an adequate prose style makes *The Western Souvenir* a worthwhile contribution to Midwestern literature.

ILLINOIS MONTHLY MAGAZINE
(1830-1832)

Hall's most ambitious project was the founding of the *Illinois Monthly Magazine*. The title was no misnomer—Illinois was its subject—and Hall's articles, tales, sketches, and current news which appeared in the magazine were chiefly indigenous. The 46-48 page monthly contained many unsigned articles. It is reasonable to assume that they were written by the editor since Hall wrote two-thirds of the material contained in the 576 pages in each volume. The practice of contributing unsigned articles, however, was common during this period. Simplicity in format with no illustrations or embellishments is characteristic of its physical features.

BLACKWELL PRINTERY

James Hall and Literary Activity

The first volume published by Robert Blackwell comprised the issues from October, 1830 to September, 1831 (Charles Keemle of St. Louis printed one issue). The second and last volume was published by Corey and Fairbank, a firm in Cincinnati, during the period from October, 1831 to September, 1832. The first year of publication merits more literary attention than the second.

Hall stated his goal in the preface of the first issue. He compared his venture to a little bark "ploughing its solitary way over the ocean." He hoped that she would be cheered with kind wishes for her safety in launching into the literary world. He invited writers to contribute; he was confident of success if they would asist him. "The leading features of our humble attempt, will be to cultivate a taste for letters, and to give correct delineation of this country to our distant friends." Hall was keenly interested in promoting interest in Western literature. Convinced that Eastern magazines were failing to give attention to books written by Westerners, he wished to do justice to these authors by developing his magazine as an instrument for nourishing letters that would utilize the frontier theme.

Unfortunately, Hall's enterprise was destined to a brief existence. Only a few writers devoted their talents to it. Difficulties were always to be encountered. The mechanical equipment and printing materials were not acquired easily. Sometimes it was necessary for the editor to suspend publication until the arrival of paper and printing ink from the East. In the March 1831 issue of the magazine Hall wrote an apology to his readers for the delay of the number. The paper shipped from Cincinnati had been delayed for three months on the river. Financial difficulties, moreover, presented a serious problem. The frontiersmen saw no reason to give three dollars for a yearly subscription to a literary periodical. The fact that Hall had courage to undertake such an enterprise is commendable.

Actually, the *Illinois Monthly Magazine* was published at a time when there was a rather extraordinary outburst of such activity which met with little success, but editors were not disturbed by the lack of either means or patronage. New Richmond, Mt. Pleasant, Oxford and Lebanon in Ohio, and Knoxville and Rogerville in Tennessee published magazines at this period. Algernon Tassin says, "Of these magazines only the Vandalia ones can be noticed." [11] In speaking of these early years, Frank Luther Mott comments, "One of the most interesting magazine files of a pioneer region is that of the *Illinois Monthly Magazine.*"[12] John T. Flanagan refers to its quality as "remarkably high" when one considers "the obstacles the editor had to overcome and the unresponsiveness of his audience."[13]

In examining the periodical, one finds that Hall obtained his goal rather well, especially in his original tales and accurate sketches of Illinois. Unfortunately, the literary reviews which Hall promised did not form a portion of each issue as he had hoped. The magazine contained, like other periodicals, a certain amount of current news, miscellaneous articles, and statistical information. Facts relating to population, commerce, bank clearing, and legislative activities furnished a certain part. Hall also followed the practice of contemporary periodicals to reprint excerpts from other magazines and newspapers.

The stories which appeared in the *Illinois Monthly Magazine* deserve emphasis since the publication was primarily a literary one. In the December 1830 issue appeared "A Legend of Carondelet," a tale of a young man Timothy Eleazer Tompkinson, posing as a physician who never presumes to exhibit any drug more active than charcoal, brickdust, or flour. This newcomer to Vide Poche, another name for Carondelet on the margin of the Mississippi, is esteemed by the women as vastly superior to the country swains in the French settlement. One is reminded of the importance that Irving's Ichabod Crane assumed among the country damsels in his "Legend of Sleepy Hollow." Hall handled the comic possibilities of superstition in much the same genial manner as Irving. Hall must have had as much fun portraying Doctor Tompkinson with his magic wheel on the rim of which were encircled cures as Irving had telling the story of the headless horseman that haunted Icabod's region. Misunderstanding evolves among the unenlightened folk of the village, Timothy loses his practice as a quack doctor, and the story concludes in an ironic twist. Hall's style strikingly resembles Irving's in its unhurried manner, vivid description, and jaunty humor. Irving was indeed the most eminent American writer at this time, and Hall, like others who followed, wrote in Irving's vein.

Hall's feeling for locale is apparent in his description of this picturesque region where the catalpa, locust, honeysuckle, and sweet brier grow luxuriantly. "A Legend of Carondelet," moreover, is one of the first attempts to record realistic dialogue. The *patois* is the broken French of M. Dunois at whose hamlet Tompkinson arrives. Hall's skill in reporting the native speech of the French and English was at a premium during a period when any attempt to record a *patois* was rare. The conversations are authentic efforts to present actuality as Hall perceived it, untouched by romantic coloring. "A Legend of Carondelet" is not only an amusing tale of the French in the New World, describing their manners and customs, but it supports the fact that Hall was employing local color before other short story writers were using this element so extensively.

"Michel de Coucy," a tale of Fort Chartres in 1750, has for its locale a French settlement in the American Bottom, "an extensive tract of rich, flat, alluvial soil which lies along the eastern shore of Mississippi and Illinois, and reaches from the river to the bluffs, and which is justly regarded as containing the greatest body of fertile land in this country, or perhaps in the universe." [14] The story concerns a Canadian boatman against whom none could pull a better oar or sing "with truer cadence the animating notes of the boat song." Michel was popular among his comrades, merry while tugging at the oar or playing the fiddle, and careful with his earnings.

Misfortunes like frost nipping his corn, cattle contracting a disease, or the loss of a boat did not upset him. To see Michel de Coucy swearing and "beating the air with his clenched fists" one day was quite an enigma to the villagers. They discovered that he had entered into a contract with Pedro Garcia and for the first time had to face a creditor. Michel had applied for a loan to the Spaniard, who readily advanced the money, making the stipulation that it was to be paid at the end of six months "with usury." When Michel did not pay at the appointed time, Garcia consulted the village civil magistrate who reasoned that if Michel did not understand the Spanish language how could he know the contents of the paper on which the loan was written.

The method of settling such differences chiefly depended on the talents of the characters rather than on legal procedure. Seizing the comedy elements in the situation at hand, Hall writes in his best vein of satire. The kidnapping of Michel's daughter by Garcia in order to compel him to pay the debt, the restoration of the lost child, and the payment of Michel's debt are narrative elements that serve to bring the story to an amusing conclusion which has no validity according to legal justice. In Michel's conviction of the validity of the settlement a satirical tone emerges, but the reader is entertained to such a degree that the satire may elude him. He feels a sense of almost personal gratitude to Hall for extricating Michel from his difficulties. The spirit of these amiable French peasants Hall has admirably captured in the pages of "Michel de Coucy," and as a result he has left an impression of French life which historians have found worthy of study.

A story that illustrates the spirit of the restless frontiersmen, dreaming of striking it rich, is "The Silver Mine." Satisfied that the Indian guide has directed him to a mine, Uncle Moses sends his cousin David to St. Louis to buy property. David's exciting ride to St. Louis, his resolutions to spend his money for the betterment of his fellowmen, his difficulties encountered, and his disappointments are related well despite the fact that Hall does not plunge immediately into his story—a fact that tends to mar the structure. Its suspenseful quality maintains a considerable tension to the very end. The amiable drifters accept gracefully the ironic twist of events.

Frequently words are italicized in "The Silver Mine"—a fact that shows Hall recognized readers did not accept vulgarity of diction. Hall uses peculiar speech turns in both dialogue and narration. The Indian setting off on a "bee line" towards the treasure, David taking a "dead aim" for St. Louis, and the characters speaking in the vernacular show that Hall is faithful to the Western scene.

Criticism was not distinctly a forte of Hall's magazine. Few books reached Vandalia, but Hall managed to review those that made their way to his desk. The literary criticism is chiefly concerned with American novels, Western books, and travel accounts by foreign visitors. Hall devoted his attention chiefly to the worthy qualities of the Western books, but one observes a hostile viewpoint toward travel accounts. In one issue he commented on thirty Americans who were attaining distinction as writers of fiction. It is obvious Hall knew which contemporary authors were artistic, for he emphasized Cooper and Irving as masters of the art. He objected strongly, however, to

Cooper's prairie scenes and to the language used by frontiersmen as unfaithful to the Western scene.

Hall hoped to see Timothy Flint's novels extensively read. He admired Flint's exploitation of Western material, namely, his realistic observations of this region, the passages devoted to the description of nature, and the attention given to Indian customs. In one issue he reviewed Flint's novel *The Shoshonee Valley* and praised "his zeal in the cause of letters."

In his review of J. C. Beltrami's *A Pilgrimage in Europe and America*, Hall resented the author's criticism of American manners. He said satirically that Beltrami took "care to record with great minuteness, all the valuable facts in relation to American manners, history, politics, etc. which he gathered from the intelligent tavern keepers, and stage drivers, who fed and forwarded him on his journey." [15]

In another issue Hall presented a scathing review of Frances Trollope's *Domestic Manners of the Americans*. He said that the accounts of the state of society and manners in this country must have been taken from some of Mrs. Trollope's associates: "From whatever sources they may have been drawn, they are certainly as new, as curious, and as wonderful to us, as they can possibly be to any of her European readers." [16] Hall assumed that the world had been favored by Mrs. Trollope's book since a certain bazaar had failed in business, referring to her unsuccessful commercial venture. Hall resented her complaints about the separation of the sexes and her reference to people who practiced chewing and smoking tobacco. He said that it was interesting to note that these Americans who live among such evils were successful in their attempts to develop resources and improve in so many things which indicate national prosperity. His only reason for noticing the book was "to attempt to arrest its demoralizing influence in our own country." According to British periodicals, the great portion of English people had been forming their judgments of Americans from her book. Hall realized that Mrs. Trollope was incapable of understanding the meaning of her observations of frontier life.

Other Americans protested loudly against her reproof which they considered an injustice. Indeed the book was anything but complimentary to American manners. Her impressions, gained largely from her residence of two years (1828-1830) in Cincinnati, were frankly expressed. Ralph Rusk, however, points out "there can be no doubt that Mrs. Trollope's strictures on Western life were almost entirely just." Social historians now contend that although the book was onesided, it was basically correct. She selected unpleasant aspects; it is obvious that she selected nothing to balance them. It was typical of Hall to defend stanchly America's national good name against a British attack.

The section devoted to poetry occupied but little space. Although it is often too stilted and ornate to achieve an artistic effect, a few contributors received recognition in *Poets and Poetry of the West,* edited by William Coggeshall in 1860. In one issue appeared Hall's poem "The Isle of the Yellow Sands," which shows his interest in Indian legends. He handled the verse and narrative element quite well. In another issue of the same year appeared his poem "The Capuchin," which shows qualities of conciseness and simplicity and an admirable handling of the ballad form.

In his various articles Hall gave prominence to the subject of a public system of education. The proportion of semi-literate people was high in this area of the West, and an academic learning in some cases was considered a handicap by frontiersmen. Working to clear the forest and providing food and shelter did not demand intellectual training. Hall saw, too, that democratic frontiersmen resented educated men who expected respect and deference. The ignorant pioneer would not be patronized. It was imperative then to stress the practicality of an education which would be an advantage rather than a hinderance. He advocated that a democracy would be stronger if its civil offices were held by men with education:

> Intelligence is power. Although in point of civil rights, all men are created equal; yet the experience of every man shows him, that those whose minds are cultivated, exert the greatest influence in society. For example, there are few offices in the state, which may be filled by men who cannot read or write, because the arts of reading and writing are necessary to the transaction of business. A man cannot be a justice of the peace, a sheriff, or a judge, without some knowledge of the law; and even if he attempts to fill inferior offices without knowing how to read, he is always acting at his peril, and in danger of being

misled by those to whom he must resort for information as to his duties.[17]

The editor strongly emphasized that competent teachers would have to be imported to Illinois because the state supported no colleges in which to train them. Those teaching seldom adopted the business as a profession. Young men who were preparing for other professions often supported themselves while pursuing other studies. He was not willing to allow the minds of Illinois children to "droop" for lack of intellectual nourishment:

> So long as we have no colleges, all the professions will be filled by young men from the eastern seminaries and while our own sons till the soil, the posts of honor will be filled by educated persons from abroad. Let us, then, cultivate education, as the means of individual and national elevation; and let us claim for Illinois, a proud standing in the literary, as well as in the political world.[18]

His cogitations often reflected this interest in education throughout the issues of the magazine. In another issue Hall maintained that the poor people of Europe had been kept in servitude and ignorance; only in Prussia, Saxony, Switzerland, Scotland, and a few other smaller districts in Europe existed systems of public education. He was quite disgruntled with many schools of England that would not confer degrees unless the recipients were *bona fide* members of the Church of England. Certainly a personal bias is apparent in his attitude toward the British, but Hall, on the whole, is capable of broad viewpoints. The reader feels he is in company with a man of deep convictions and of an astute and sympathetic mind and a writer of clear, effective, and convincing prose. Indeed Hall deserves to be remembered as one of the vigorous advocates of public education.

The relations of the government with the Indian tribes were a subject increasing in importance. In a series of four issues the editor discusses the "ruinous tendency of the policy now pursued, and the absolute necessity of a speedy and radical change." He advocated giving the Indian full possession of the rights of self-government and not restraining him from the sale of his land to any people but Americans. Rejecting the Indian as a degraded creature was a serious fault of Americans. It was unjust to adopt a policy founded on the principle that the red man was only "ferocious, ignorant and brutal" while the white man was "civilized and polished." Since Americans had united to encourage a new type of living for mankind, it was unfortunate to note in their relation that "one little remnant of the human family stands unaffected."

Hall examined the events leading up to this disposition of feeling toward the Indian. He believed that the real acts of cruelty were committed by the white men. The Indians had possessed a high moral character in their primitive state, but civilized men had poisoned the Indian mind by breaking faith with them. The greatest fault lay in the inept handling of the situation and the corrupt practices of the white men. Furthermore, Americans disregarded government laws forbidding them to trespass upon Indian hunting grounds, and often they destroyed vast quantities of game. The Indians entertained, until this abuse, a friendly disposition toward Americans. The editor concluded with a hopeful note that Americans would hear the evidence and the "question to be decided will be, whether the savage tribes shall be driven beyond our frontiers, and left to their fate, or be subjected to the wholesome constraint of our laws." It is interesting to note today that ideas presented by Hall have been incorporated into the policies of the government but unfortunately not until the twentieth century. Critics, on the whole, disagree with Hall's rather romantic conception of the savage. Nevertheless, his attitude has been recognized. Hall is convincing and sincere in crusading for justice to the Indian.

The editor's serial "Notes on Illinois" occupied an important section of the magazine. In one issue Hall described the topography. The settlers found themselves surrounded by one vast prairie except near streams and rivers which were "fringed with strips of woodland." It was the annual burning of the prairies which destroyed the young timber within its range. Fires stopped at the margin of streams where the soil was moist. Hall described the American Bottom, which Charles Dickens pictured years later in his travel book *American Notes*. Hall said that it commenced some distance below Kaskaskia and extended ninety miles up the Mississippi River. He believed the scenery on the Mississippi surpassed that on the Ohio in its beauty, its richness, and its variety of landscape. Most travelers and reporters preferred the beauty of the Ohio River.

In another issue in his "Notes on Illinois," Hall devoted his attention to flowers and fruits. The wild honeysuckle, roses, and violets flourished luxuriantly. Lilacs bloomed profusely. Fruits were remarkably fine. Apples were especially large and well-flavored. Pears, quinces, cherries, gooseberries, currants, raspberries, and strawberries grew without much attention to their culture—"scarcely any beyond the art of planting." Hall was impressed with the fertility of the soil which was "of unrivalled depth, fertility, and freshness."

Hall mentioned in another issue the wild animals that were still roaming Illinois in their native freedom. Previously the state had afforded pasturage to large herds of buffalo. In 1831 only the traces of buffalo—the well-beaten tracks—remained. Deer was quite plentiful. He mentioned while sitting at the door of a log cabin one evening he heard the wolves chasing the deer. Venison hams and hides were important articles of import. At Vandalia hams were purchased from the hunters at "something like one cent a pound." Elk had disappeared, bear and beaver were seldom seen, but the fox, panther, and wolf were still roaming the prairies. The raccoon and the opossum, plundering cornfields and attacking poultry, were troublesome to the farmer, the rabbits were destructive to the orchards and gardens, and polecats also destroyed poultry. There were no rats in Vandalia; none appeared in Illinois except along the large rivers where the boats had landed.

Hall discusses the laws of Illinois in another issue. The courts were then modeled chiefly upon the judiciary system of Kentucky. Candidates for admission to the bar were examined personally by two judges of the Supreme Court. A license permitted one to practice law in any court in the state. No particular term of study or of residence was prescribed, but testimonials of good moral character were required.

Negroes, Indians, and mulattoes were not allowed to be witnesses in court against a white person. The point was clarified that this area was not a retreat for free Negroes or runaway slaves. Every Negro coming into the state to reside had to file documentary evidence of his freedom in the office of the circuit clerk of the county in which he intended to live and give bond which entailed security for his good behavior and maintenance. Such facts were presented objectively. But Hall obviously felt strongly about gambling and duelling. In the seat of government several acts were passed to punish gambling which Hall referred to as a "detestable vice." Those who engaged in duelling in any manner could not qualify to hold any office of trust and profit in civil or military matters.

A series of articles on emigration illustrate the value of the magazine as an organ of information about the frontier. Hall listed the prices of food in the January 1832 issue thereby showing the abundance and relatively low cost. Eggs were selling for 6½ to 12 cents a dozen. The following prices were per bushel: apples, 50 cents; potatoes, 15 to 25 cents; turnips, 12½ to 15 cents. Honey sold at 50 cents a gallon, and butter at 6¼ to 15 cents per pound. Turkeys brought 12½ cents apiece, and chickens cost 75 cents to $1 per dozen. Beef, pork, and venison hams were also selling at relatively low prices. Farming in primitive fashion was on a small scale, but the agricultural products of the Middle West were, in time, to feed the whole country. Hall was convinced of the potentialities of this region. He believed that the fertile soil, mineral resources, and central location of Illinois in relation to the American continent were all conducive to the growth of agriculture, industry, and commerce. The people of Illinois longed to see the productive plains covered with "an industrious, an enterprising, and an intelligent population." Foreigners must leave behind them their prejudices and many of their customs which would be inappropriate to this country. The climate and soil being new to them, they would have to remodel their system of agriculture. The man who came without money or friends, expecting to find them in Illinois, was the person who intended to stay. Hall advised that the best seasons to emigrate to Illinois were spring and autumn. Emigrants traveling in summer or winter would be exposed to the extremes of heat and cold. Transportation by water was preferable. Emigrants arriving by way of the Ohio River could disembark at Shawneetown and take a stage to Vandalia. Hall, like Birkbeck, wrote enthusiastically about the region, rarely mentioning an inconvenience or hardship.

The *Illinois Monthly Magazine* has left a vivid and authentic account of the settlement of the early West. Such material would have doubtless been lost had it not been preserved within the pages of Hall's periodical. After two years of a relatively unsuccessful fight to maintain a literary magazine in the wilderness of Illinois, James

Hall relinquished his position as editor, publisher, and owner. The magazine was a financial failure with considerable loss to its editor. Historically, James Hall's *Illinois Monthly Magazine* was successful. He has left to Illinois two volumes which critics recognize as a literary achievement in the frontier area.

LEGENDS OF THE WEST

In 1832 Hall published the book *Legends of the West*, perhaps the most valuable of all his work. This volume includes three short stories "A Legend of Carondelet," "Michel de Coucy," and "The Indian Hater" and two poems "The Indian Wife's Lament" and "The Isle of the Yellow Sands"—all of which had previously appeared in his Vandalia periodical or annual. He included five tales which had not appeared in print at Vandalia. Hall's prefatory statement indicates the type of material to be found in the volume:

> The legends now presented to the public are entirely ficti-
> tious; but they are founded upon incidents which have been
> witnessed by the author during a long residence in the western
> states, or upon traditions preserved by the people, and have
> received but little artificial embellishment.

Certainly Hall knew his position as recorder of frontier life. Instruction invariably accompanies the entertainment in his stories. The firstcomers in every frontier were the backwoodsmen. They inhabited the Vandalia area before the commissioners decided upon the spot for the capital. Morris Birkbeck had described backwoods-men as finding "the regulations of society intolerable." Wealth, family, or position in life meant nothing to these early settlers. In "The Backwoodsmen," the first tale, Hall records a clear account of this type.

> They lived in cabins hastily erected for temporary shelter,
> and as hastily abandoned when a slight allurement at some
> distant spot invited them to change their residence. Their per-
> sonal effects were of course few, and their domestic utensils rude
> and simple. Their horses, their rifles, and their herds, constituted
> their wealth; and with these they were prepared at a moment's
> warning to push farther into the wilderness, selling their habi-
> tations for a mere trifle, or abandoning them to any chance
> occupant who might choose to take possession, and conquering
> for themselves a new home, from the panther and the Indian.[19]

Another story included in this volume is "The Seventh Son," which concerns Jeremy Geode, the seventh son of an Indian doctor, who had the power to cure diseases by means of the Kickapoo Panacea. The story is based upon the belief of frontiersmen that a seventh son was blessed with rare skill. Hall handles the legend with his usual polish, realistic touches of local color, and humor.

Hall could well have been describing the primitive settlement of Vandalia when he first saw it, with one exception. The village was not composed of only log cabins. He was articulate and faithful to fact in both his description of locale and in his observations of the firstcomers.

> Doctor Geode settled in an obscure town, far in the wilderness. It was a village newly laid out, upon the borders of an extensive prairie; a beautifully undulating plain, fringed with woods, and dotted with picturesque clumps and groves of trees. The grass, as yet but little trodden, exhibited its pristine luxuriance, and a variety of gorgeous flowers enlivened the scene. The deer still loitered here, as if unwilling to resign their ancient pastures, and at night the long howl of the wolf could be heard, mingled with the fearful screechings of the owl. The village was composed of log cabins, and was, with the neighbourhood around it, inhabited chiefly by backwoodsmen—a race of people who, delighting in the chase, and devoted to their wild, free, and independent habits, precede the advance of the denser population, and keep ever on the outskirts of society. Ardent, hospitable, and uncultivated, the stranger is as much delighted with the cordial welcome he finds at their fireside, as he is struck with their primitive manners, their singular phraseology, and their original modes of thinking.[20]

An example of Hall's humor that flickers through the narrative is the comment concerning Jeremy Geode.

> "He loved books, I loved men—particularly those of the feminine gender. He was devoted to figures, and so was I—but then his affection settled upon the figures of arithmetic and geometry, while mine were running riot among those of the cotillion."[21]

Other tales, besides those already mentioned, that appeared in *Legends of the West* are "The Divining Rod," "The Missionaries," "The Intestate," "The Emigrants," and "The Barrack-master's Daughter." It is indeed remarkable that a volume of short stories had appeared in Midwestern letters as early as 1832 when the short story as an art form was merely a novel undertaking not to be taken

138

seriously as a type of literature. *Legends of the West* remains a valuable contribution to early American literature.

A tragedy which occurred in Hall's life at Vandalia was the death of his wife and infant son James. So little has been written about Mary Posey Hall, who was born in Virginia, January 22, 1799, yet she was the inspiration of at least one of Hall's poems "To Mary." She died August 18, 1832.

As state treasurer Hall competently reorganized the financial system. He was not reappointed to the position because of his loyalty to William Kinney and his antagonism to Governor Reynolds. In 1833 he removed to Cincinnati where he spent the rest of his life. For two years he edited the *Western Monthly Magazine*. In September, 1839, he married Mary Louisa Alexander, a widow. Hall continued to publish his writings, namely, *The Soldier's Bride and Other Tales* (1833); *the Harpe's Head* (1833); *The Western Reader; a Series of Useful Lessons* (1833); *Sketches of History, Life, and Manners in the West* (1834); *Tales of the Border* (1835); *Statistics of the West, At the Close of the Year 1836*, (1836); *The Wilderness and the Warpath* (1846); and *History of the Indian Tribes of North America* (1836-1844). His last published writing appeared in 1857. From that time he devoted his attention to banking until his death July 5, 1868.

Such was the writing career of an American whom no one has surpassed as a recorder and interpreter of early Illinois history, life, and legend. And it was this author who spent his most active years in Vandalia to which town he brought literary recognition. But he is more than a local author. Hall's writings must be classed among the literary influences of American letters during the birth of a national literature. It is Hall's faults in writing that have caused some critics to neglect his short stories. Construction is a weakness, his plots are defective, and his style to a certain degree suffers from diffuseness and lack of compactness. Hall made a contribution, nonetheless, to the formative period of the short story. His descriptions of the prairies were among the first extensive, accurate ones included in American literature. Today he is considered an authoritative writer of the West. He preserved a record of the types of frontiersmen before unheeded. Realistic dialogue, which had rarely been done, he employed, and he used American speech to develop American themes. He did not fail to provide the West with a regional literature that compared well with the East. He was a pioneer in the field of realism, moving definitely in that direction and clearing the path for more successful realists. James Hall unquestionably deserves his niche in the development of the American short story.

James Hall's name is inscribed in memory in the Berry-Hall Room of the Little Brick House. Material concerning him and his work is being compiled there. An original book by James Hall recommends itself to the attention of visitors; *Statistics of the West*, published in Cincinnati in 1836, contains some material first printed in his Vandalia magazine. The table of contents indicates its nature. As one may guess from these topics—topography of the valley of the Mississippi, the Ohio River, the prairies, wild animals, birds, flowers, western steamboats, trade and commerce—, the basic purpose is presentation of a tabular account of conditions of the early West. Such is the only book by James Hall that remains in Vandalia to which town the author left a legacy of culture. Hall's portrait, the frontier character Pete Featherton, and the Blackwell Printery—all sketches that appear on the folk-art map, his name on the map of Illinois Authors, and a pencil portrait serve to commemorate the talents of Vandalia's first author and the early West's most distinguished writer.

JAMES HALL AND LITERARY ACTIVITY

1. Flanagan, **James Hall,** op. cit., pp. 9-10
2. Merle Curti, **The Growth of American Thought** (New York, 1951), p. 277
3. James Hall, **Western Souvenir** (Cincinnati, 1828), pp. 263-264
4. Ibid., p. 57
5. Ibid., p. 106
6. Ibid., pp. 10-11
7. Ibid., pp. 251-252
8. All four poems are available in the Berry-Hall Room of the Little Brick House.
9. Van Wycke Brooks **The World of Washington Irving** (Philadelphia, 1945), p. 462
10. Dumas Malone (Ed.), **Dictionary of American Biography,** Vol. IV (New York, 1932), p. 172
11. Algernon Tassin, **The Magazine of America** (New York, 1916), p. 201
12. Frank Mott, **A History of American Magazines 1741-1850** (New York, 1930), p. 595
13. Flanagan, op. cit., p. 60
14. **Illinois Monthly Magazine,** December 1830, p. 102
15. Ibid., June 1831, p. 426
16. Ibid., August 1832, p. 506
17. Ibid., December 1830, p. 112
18. Ibid., December 1830, p. 121
19. James Hall, **Legends of the West** (Philadelphia, 1833), p. 4
20. Ibid., pp. 75-76
21. Ibid., p. 68

CONTEMPORARY ART EXPRESSIVE OF HISTORY

THE MADONNA OF THE TRAIL STATUE

A visitor to an old American town does not expect to find an ancient fortress, or a castle on a lofty hill overlooking the village, or a cathedral whose spire dominates the landscape. It has something else to offer in true American fashion. The white man has pushed out the native Indian, cleared the woodland, and plowed the prairie. In its place he has built a town and on its fringes he has cultivated the land into farms. Such is Vandalia but with a distinction that sets it apart from other old prairie towns in Illinois. Besides its historical significance, it has a statue such as no other town in the state possesses. It symbolizes the frontier woman who helped to explore a virgin land. The statue on the southwest corner of the Statehouse lawn is a solid memento of brave and perservering women who struggled for an existence in their new home of adoption. It impresses on the soul a certain feeling of solemn determination that must have been exhibited to a marked degree in the pioneer women who came west.

The statue of the frontier mother was presented to the state of Illinois in October, 1928, by the Daughters of the American Revolution. It is one of twelve erected by this organization in each state through which the National Old Trails Road ran. The society sought to express in this manner its appreciation of the sacrifices made by pioneer mothers. The decision to place the statue in Illinois offered no difficulty since Vandalia was the logical spot. The National Road, built by the Federal Government to the early West, began in Cumberland, Maryland, ran through Ohio, Indiana, and terminated in Vandalia, Illinois.

The sculptor August Leimbach, born in Kallennordheim, Germany, turned to his most noted creation outside the realm of architectural sculpture when he produced the eighteen-foot statue out of Missouri Algonite granite. Leimbach received his training in the art of sculpture in Stuttgart and Hamburg. In 1910 he came to St.

Louis to reside. It was here that Mrs. John Trigg Moss, a national officer in the Daughters of the American Revolution, contacted the sculptor. In collaboration with her son John Trigg Moss, Jr., she designed the monument which Leimbach sculptured.

Olivia Leidig Whiteman, who unveiled the statue, was in 1928 the only living Vandalia resident that actually knew Abraham Lincoln. When she was visiting her aunt in Springfield, Lincoln invited her to go with Tad and him to a circus. She often recalled the happy times that she had playing with Tad. Her favorite recollection of Tad was his hiding under the bed and waiting for his father to find him. Lincoln would cheerfully acquiesce to his caper, go to the bed, and call, "Come on out, monkey Tad." [1] This quiet, gentle lady was especially shy when in the limelight simply because she had known the Lincoln family.

It was this little lady who maintained firmly in her soft-spoken voice that Mrs. Lincoln had been misrepresented to the public. When Joseph Burtschi introduced her to Ida Tarbell, who had written the two volumes *Life of Abraham Lincoln*, the author inquired about Mrs. Lincoln's treatment of her husband. Entreaties were useless. Olivia Whiteman repeatedly answered to every question, "Mrs. Lincoln was a very nice woman." [2] Her heart knew only kindness, not abasement, for her friend.

Besides her association with the Lincolns, Olivia Whiteman was a capital descendant. Her parents, George and Sophia Remann Leidig, were members of the Ernst Colony. Her mother brought with her a china figurine resembling the Madonna of the Trail inasmuch as it represented a woman, her child, and a dog at her skirts. Her son George referred to the three-piece china object as a thimble holder. Others maintain the "Sophia Doll," as it is affectionately called, is a candle holder. Regardless of its identification, many observe a marked resemblance between the statue and the china figurine.

Olivia Whiteman unveiled the Madonna of the Trail in her modest, unpretentious manner before a crowd of ten thousand who attended the impressive dedication ceremonies. Frank A. Davis, who spoke in the absence of Judge Harry S. Truman of Independence, Missouri, said, "There are other great national highways, but there are none of them that are permeated with the history and sentiment

that abounds along the course of this one." [3] Mrs. John Trigg Moss'
dedicatory words were, "Vandalia was intimately associated with the
early romantic history of this section of our country—and it is fitting
that we shall place here, upon such sacred soil, our beloved memorial
of the past." [4]

MADONNA OF THE TRAIL

The colorful pageant parade consisted of pioneer covered wagons,
pony-riding Indians, trappers in buckskin breeches and coonskin
caps, horseback riders, stagecoaches, costumed men and women, and
men garbed as Lincoln, Douglas, and other legislators. A host of
youngsters, dressed as Indians, formed a sizable chorus at the monument. The great mass of people saw the enactment of a scene that
represented a significant part of Vandalia's rich heritage—the

meeting of Lincoln and Douglas for the first time. The celebration was the "most colorful, best organized, and largest attended" of the unveilings held in the eight states where the memorials were erected reported the secretary of the road association, Frank A. Davis.

The monument fondly bears on the pedestal an inscription that boasts of Lincoln's association with Vandalia:

AT VANDALIA ABRAHAM LINCOLN,
MEMBER OF THE ILLINOIS LEGISLATURE,
FIRST FORMULAT3D
THOSE HIGH PRINCIPLES
OF FREEDOM AND JUSTICE
WHICH GAVE THE SLAVES
A LIBERATOR
THE UNION A SAVIOUR

Norval Gochenour had been asked to write an inscription relative to Vandalia's importance in the history of the National Road. He studied for days on the assignment but was dissatisfied with his attempt. He felt that his wording was inadequate for the purpose. Finally he asked Samuel Brooks Murray, a man interested in Vandalia's history, to write an inscription. [5] Murray's words are engraved on another side of the pedestal:

THE CUMBERLAND ROAD
BUILT BY
THE FEDERAL GOVERNMENT
WAS AUTHORIZED BY CONGRESS
AND APPROVED BY
THOMAS JEFFERSON IN 1806.
VANDALIA MARKS THE
WESTERN TERMINUS

The visitor's mind returns to an earlier age as he views the statue. Jefferson's authorization of the road in 1806 clearly indicated that the Alleghenies would no longer offer a barrier between the Atlantic Coast and the Western states. The War of 1812 had demonstrated the need for national roads, but allowing appropriation to the Cumberland Road became a constitutional question. It appeared upon President Madison's election in 1816 that the road would not be finished to Vandalia. Although the measure for the costs of building the National Road had passed the House, Madison vetoed it on constitutional grounds. In 1822 Madison vetoed an act to establish tollgates on the road. Despite such opposition, a bill appropriating

144

funds passed in 1824. It was Albert Gallatin, Secretary of the Treasury, who vigorously applied his efforts to sending the road to Vandalia. In 1828 the road was under construction in Illinois. The unveiling of the statue in 1928 was also an occasion for celebrating the centennial of the National Road in Illinois.

Only a trace existed before the road was constructed through the bottom land east of Vandalia. George Flower, Birkbeck's partner in the English settlement of Albion, speaks of the so-called road leading to Vandalia as a track made by men on horseback. "Before getting to Vandalia," Flower says, "there was a low piece of timbered bottom-land, wet and swampy, and often covered with water, through which every traveler had to make his way best he could, often at the risk of his life." [6]

Flower also relates an experience which happened to three lawyers traveling by horseback to Vandalia in the 1820's. Judge Wilson, Samuel Lockwood, and Henry Eddy rode from the direction of Shawneetown on a winter day without seeing any signs of human habitation. The weather became very cold, and a heavy snowfall added to their peril. They were compelled to spend the night on the open prairies, terrified lest they should freeze to death before morning. It was before noon the next day that the three reached the east bank of the Kaskaskia River, which was at flood water stage. The men swam their horses across and arrived at Vandalia, dripping wet, in the frigid air. Lockwood resigned himself to his destiny, thinking the exposure would prove fatal, but after a short illness he recovered. Such were the hazardous traveling conditions that placed pioneers in jeopardy of their lives.

In 1828 the mile stretch through the bottom land east of the Kaskaskia River was still heavily timbered. It was a tremendous undertaking clearing the sixty-six foot strip through underbrush and forest trees of such gigantic size. The roadbed itself was only thirty feet wide. Both oxen and horses were used to pull the huge stumps around which chains were fastened. The workers grumbled; it was too much physical exertion and they felt they were poorly paid. A song or rhyme that has been handed down describes the wretched condition of the pike:

Vandalia: Wilderness Capital of Lincoln's Land

The roads are impassable—
Hardy jackassable;
I think those that travel 'em
Should turn out and gravel 'em.[7]

Past the Statehouse Square rolled the wheels of Conestoga wagons carrying settlers into a new life and hauling freight into a frontier territory and stagecoaches carrying travelers who would view the new land and then return home to sing its praises or to disparage the glowing accounts that had been written about it. A parade of critical visitors wanting to see the new democracy at work on the frontier came through Vandalia. Many were convinced that the emotional religion at the camp meetings, the insolence of servants, and the free-for-alls in the grog-shops were too much for the educated man to tolerate. Travelers often jotted down their observations in a crusty, caustic prose. The impressions of the road and of the town recorded by these travelers is a part of Vandalia history.

In October, 1835, Frederick Gustorf, a young German intellectual, reported a forest on both sides of the road to the banks of the river. He referred to the building of the National Road as a "gigantic task" because of the shortage of funds and labor. The newspaper printed notices that seven hundred workmen were needed on the road. He found only four busy on a mile stretch where forty should have been working. To Gustorf the town was "dark and depressing" and would certainly disintegrate if plans to remove the capital materialized. The swampy land east of the river and signs of disease on the inhabitants' faces indicated to him an unhealthy climate. A recent suicide of a young German who apparently found living in Vandalia impossible and Gustorf's conversation with the widow and daughter of Ferdinand Ernst convinced him that the town was unbearable. Gustorf spent the night at the Vandalia Inn where the "bed was free of bugs" (such was the only bright spot in the otherwise gloomy remarks of his journal). His expenses totaled one dollar for the overnight stay which included three meals.[8]

Edmund Flagg's description is another acrid account of Vandalia. He spoke of it as "a miserable town withered like a flower in the prairie heat at noon." Since Flagg was a schoolmaster trained in the classics, he appreciated the fact that Vandalia offered a literary periodical of such creditable writing. He referred to the *Illinois Monthly Magazine* as an "ably-conducted publication." During the summer of 1836 Flagg stopped at Vandalia on his "ramble over the prairies." Soon a series of articles under the title "Sketches of a Traveller" by Flagg appeared in the periodical *Louisville Journal.* Later in 1838 Flagg's impressions on his pilgrimage appeared in two volumes entitled *The Far West: or A Tour Beyond the Mountains.* Vandalia is described in the first volume.

William Oliver, a British visitor in 1841, saw the road under construction east of Vandalia. He commented about some stumps that were still there and how the road was blocked in parts by fences built by the local farmers. One incident that involves rather amusing frontier speech could have happened at the old National Road inn where the Vincennes Road meets the Cumberland Road.

"Not far from Vandalia, Oliver drew rein to water his horse at an execrable well. As he slipped off the bridle, he heard two natives talking.

'How you gettin' on?' asked the first.

The other shook his head. 'Well, I can't tell. I think I'll move.'

'Move, why?'

'Well, the country is gettin' so peopled up, I can't live in it no how.'

'Why the last time I saw you, you told me your next neighbor lived seven miles off.'

'Yes, but there is one within three miles now, and I can't stand it no longer. One can't go out into the woods but he hears the sound of the ax and the crash of trees.' " [9]

The backwoodsmen actually resented the arrival of new settlers. The farmer welcomed them, seizing the chance to enjoy their companionship. He offered help to build the newcomer's log cabin, but the backwoodsmen preferred to exist without the conditions of society imposed upon him. It is quite probable that the "execrable well" to which Oliver referred was the one offered travelers for their horses and oxen in the yard of the inn.

It has been reported that the two-story brick structure of Georgian architecture that stands at the confluence of the National and

Vincennes Road was an old inn to accommodate travelers. The architecture is bulky and rugged with a sense of old pioneer strength. Similar to other early structures of this area it is without adornment, except the front veranda. It is logical that the structure served as an inn during capital days as its location is at the meeting of two vital thoroughfares. Furthermore, rarely is found on the prairies a large, old brick building in a rural area. The Vincennes Road made its way through Mt. Vernon and Salem, coming in a northwesterly direction from the south. It is now almost dozing—so drowsy that one seldom recalls its early importance when it clamored with traffic from Shawneetown. The primitive roadside inn, stripped of its one time spirited activity, reminds the visitor of a by-gone age when Conestoga wagons lumbered along the pioneer highways.

The "execrable well" of which Oliver speaks was probably not the Twin Pumps on the Cumberland Road, located six miles east of Vandalia. Ezra Griffith, who came to this area in 1830, built the first frame house in Cumberland Township. The building, erected in 1835, contained the Cumberland Post Office, a store, and living quarters for the Griffith family. Across the road on the north side stood the wooden Twin Pumps with a horse trough, hewn out of logs, at each one. The pump on the inside of the fence was used by the Griffith family for stock; the other on the outside of the fence was used by the traveler. Mr. Griffith maintained the pumps and provided a tin cup for the traveler to use. On the south side of the road for a quarter of a mile extended a line of shady locust trees. Here the traveler stopped to water his horses and to rest under the shade.[10] At the Griffith Corner today a barn stands north of the site of the Twin Pumps, and a modern house has been built on the site of the old frame structure.

Another building that stood on the Cumberland Road in the early days is no longer in existence. About one mile east of the Kaskaskia River is the site of a tollhouse which was still standing in the 1870's. Since drivers of stagecoaches and freight-wagons derisively referred to it as a "privy," it might be that it resembled a shanty rather than a graceful structure like the tollhouses in the East. On the other hand, such a name may have been directed to it only to show resentment toward payment of toll or inconvenience of stopping. Only one connection with the tollhouse has been related to the author. In the latter nineteenth century Vandalians enjoyed a Sunday afternoon ride in their buggies as far as the tollhouse. [11] But even in the relating of that usual pastime, one was aware that the tollhouse was not a general favorite among the users of the Cumberland Road.

A road made of wooden planks laid transversely for a single passage of a wagon was constructed on the bottom land stretch. It was built on an elevation of dirt dug from the Dollar Hole, the sunken area located north of the Victor Clark house, named for the fact that each laborer received a dollar a day for digging and loading the dirt in wagons to haul to the road. [12]

According to congressional specifications, the bridges were to be of stone, but on the last mile stretch they were built of wood. Greenup maintained that it was not practicable to finish the grubbing and provide no means to cross the ditches and river. In his communications to Washington he begged action. It was not until 1840 that a covered bridge spanned the Kaskaskia. It is reported that another covered bridge to which a chain was attached to prevent entrance stood at the edge of the Clark property. Toll was collected at this point. One resident of Vandalia said that she could not recall whether the toll was collected at the bridge or whether there was a tollhouse. It was discovered after a flood in 1931 that the abutments built by Greenup's road crew did not satisfactorily divert the pressure of moving water. The bridges were extended, and the stones from the supporting structures were removed to the lake dam and waterfall at the Evans acreage on which the log cabin stands. Modern bridges now span the ditches on the bottom land east of the river. The four-lane bridge, completed in 1963, is the fourth one to be built across the Kaskaskia on the Cumberland Road.

On the west bank of the Kaskaskia high on the north bluff is located an original tollhouse which in the early days stood down on the road. The white frame of many-paned windows was also the home of William Shelton, toll collector. A chain fastened to a post was drawn across the covered bridge to prevent travelers from passing without paying. One evening some chap sawed the post to the ground. [13] Vandalians protested the collecting of toll, as did President Monroe, on the grounds that it was unconstitutional. The point of toll collection was then transferred to the covered bridge over the dredge ditch. Driving into Vandalia, visitors pass unknowingly the only tollhouse left on the National Road in Illinois.

The National Road, which extended 591 miles from Cumberland to Vandalia, cost the government approximately seven million dollars. It is a symbol of the strength and serious concern of the national government for unity between the East and West. Indeed it has its many places of storied charm, but at the terminus, where the statue stands, the visitor may become more aware of its significance. In the phrasing of Joseph Burtschi, "The route has historical interest second to no other in the United States." [14]

THE CAPITAL MURAL

The appearance of Vandalia in 1836 is depicted in a mural that is located in the dining room of Hotel Evans. Joseph Burtschi desired to see a reproduction of the town displayed for visitors to view. He had assembled a number of faded photographs and sketches of original buildings drawn by early settlers, and he knew where these structures were located on the square during the capital period. Present-day historians often give the impression that Vandalia was a settlement of log cabins in 1836. To be sure there was a smattering of such humble structures, but the streets were not lined with them. Directly west of the old Aragon Hotel, however, there stood two or three log cabins occupied by Negroes who had been brought to Vandalia and freed by their owners. The brick and frame buildings were huge in comparison to the neighboring settlements. In fact, to some travelers they were of such immense size that the town presented an unnatural aspect, considering the limited extension of its boundaries. Such a mural, then, would shed light on the appearance of the capital. Joseph Burtschi took his idea to Charles Evans, who agreed to bear the financial burden of the enterprise.

The painting, eight by seventeen foot and three inches, is the work of John Matthew Heller, who followed in precise detail the instructions of Joseph Burtschi, who engaged in exhaustive research in order to render the mural as authentic as possible. There may be more vital sheen, picturesqueness, and quaint charm, and cleaner and better kept buildings—the poetic license of the painter—than one found in the frontier world, but the reproduction is authentic. The painting was dedicated in October, 1954.

The Statehouse without its Doric piers in the center of the painting faces south. To the right, across the street east, is a small white frame that served as the post office. North of it is a two-story log hotel built by Frederick Hollman for Ferdinand Ernst in 1819. Immediately behind the Statehouse is the two-story white frame residence of Robert McLaughlin where Governor Bond lived during legislative sessions. Directly east is located the House of Divine Worship. Directly west of the McLaughlin homestead is the Ebenezer Capps store, largest in southern Illinois at the time. This store had the reputation of keeping everything. One newly-elected legislator took the bet that he could mention an item not found at Capps' store. He asked for goose yokes. Capps promptly supplied them, chuckling that he always kept them for the lawmakers. In front of the store is a clerk, showing a customer the true color of a piece of yard-goods in the daylight. This store, known from here to New Orleans, established prices for commodities throughout the southern part of the state. Directly north of the store is the bull pen, the place for settling arguments physically. The rowdies could brawl here without damaging the dignity of the capital square. Across the street was the jail where the Methodist Church now stands. South of the jail and across the street west of Capps' store is the Green Tree Hotel, which was operated by Thomas Redmond.

On the corner in the left foreground is the Chartres Hotel on the site of the present-day Hotel Evans. North of the Chartres is the Anthenaeum, which served as a theatre. An imaginative meeting between Lincoln and Douglas occurs on Gallatin Street in front of the Chartres. Across the street is the Mathew Duncan Hotel on the corner. Duncan, a lawyer, was founder of the first Illinois newspaper —the Illinois *Herald*, 1814, in Kaskaskia. It was in this hotel that James Stuart, author of *Three Years in North America*, secured a room in 1830. Duncan, wishing to supply information for his British guest, contacted Mary Hall, who sent her little daughter to the hotel with some of her husband's publications. Judge Hall was out of town at the time. Robert Blackwell also furnished some Vandalia newspapers for the visitor to read. Both men were no doubt eager to provide the writer with another aspect of Vandalia life besides the grog-shops. Travelers often emphasized the smoking, drinking, fighting, and hullabaloo heard from these public places. Stuart's opinion of Vandalia's culture, however, was one of admiration. The proceedings of the historical society particularly impressed him as extraordinary, and into his book went the favorable reaction.

At the left of the hotel is the Blackwell Printery. Directly across the street on the east to the right is the Vandalia Hotel. The small building at the extreme left, facing south, is the birthplace of the research historian for the mural. Directly east of this home is the Morey Building. At the extreme lower right of the painting is the Thompson's Tavern, commonly called the Vandalia Inn, which served as the headquarters for the Overland Stage Company. Directly west of the inn is the State Bank Building—the one which travelers described as incongruous among the other plain structures on the square. It was a two-story brick with massive pillars.

John Matthew Heller, born in St. Louis, Missouri, studied at the Cincinnati Art School in Ohio, School of Fine Arts at Washington University in St. Louis, and the Pennsylvania Academy in Philadelphia. In Europe he studied at the Julian Academy in Paris and the Royal Academies in Munich and London. He has designed and executed murals both in the states and abroad and has painted portraits and genre compositions—many for which he has won awards. His outstanding work in recent years is a series of steamboat paintings. He maintains a studio in St. Louis, and since 1954 he frequently visits Vandalia, the town he built on canvas.

The artist enjoys telling a story about the research historian. At first the jail was a frame structure. He painted it as such. No, on further research the jail was built of stone. While the artist was in the process of painting it as a stone structure, the historian hurriedly sent word that the jail was constructed of brick. "If you change the material one more time, I'll put you in that jail!" the artist exploded. [15]

Another problem was drawing the sweep which the historian requested. How could one sketch a sweep on a well when he had no idea what it looked like? Every person whom the artist asked in St.

152

Louis thought it was probably a kind of broom to sweep out the well. The historian, amused that such a simple thing appeared menacing and insolvable to the artist, offered no help except the suggestion to explore the library to which Heller betook himself and found the answer. But such difficulty was nothing compared to moving the buildings from one place to another. The jail and bull pen were moved several times. At first the Statehouse was placed in the center, but the historian's birthplace must be on the mural so the capitol was moved to the right somewhat so the little one-story house could be squeezed into the picture.

Indeed the artist with his deft strokes has given life and movement to the primitive capital. The center of interest is the Statehouse to which everything leads: the stage coach, wagons, and horses are all headed toward it. The simplicity of the lawn gives center fielding to the staccato (the red with the white-framed windows) of the Statehouse. The historian was not certain that a picket fence surrounded the square so the artist left it out; it would have nonetheless cluttered the picture. There were probably more trees than painted, but they would have hindered the view of the buildings. The mural is made of the finest materials. The canvas was imported from England. The colors, purchased from France, Germany, England, and Holland, will never fade. The primary colors were used. The important things are in red. Towards the top, the landscape becomes less distinct and here the painter used blues and violets. Such is the quality and remarkable coloring of this work of art cherished by Vandalians.

The visitor realizes after he has seen the mural and the historic sights of Vandalia that the once obscure lawmaker from Sangamon County is not the only subject worthy of attention in the old capital. William Baringer has grasped the significance and expressed it adequately:

> If deprived of its Lincoln connection the story of the rise and fall of Vandalia, pioneer capital, and its legislative sessions, would still be well worth the telling as social history. There one can see, in microcosm, the growth and functioning of American pioneer government and the early American town.[16]

Vandalia: Wilderness Capital of Lincoln's Land

Vandalia, assigned to the enterprise of government, was a hopeful venture for the future of modern democracy. It is mainly from reading the story of Vandalia that the American can feel a well-grounded sense of pride in his government and in his country. The problems, the decisions, and the long-range implications which faced the legislators at the state capital possessed both national and local importance. Indeed a meaningful experience awaits the visitor who will find his way to the very epitome of the pioneer American village—Vandalia.

CONTEMPORARY ART EXPRESSIVE OF HISTORY

1. George L. Whitman by interview supplied the information.
2. J. C. Burtschi by interview supplied the information. When Ida M. Tarbell came to Vandalia in November, 1922, to secure information for her book **In The Footsteps of the Lincolns**, J. C. Burtschi, mayor, acted as host to the writer.
3. Vandalia **Union**, Nov. 1, 1928.
4. Vandalia **Leader**, Nov. 1, 1928.
5. C. A. Evans by interview supplied the information.
6. Flower, **op. cit.**, p. 12
7. Philip D. Jordan, **The National Road** (New York, 1948), p. 136
8. Fred Gustorf, "Frontier Perils Told by an Early Illinois Visitor," **Journal**, Ill. State Hist. Soc., LV, (Summer, 1962), pp. 152-154.
9. Jordan, **op. cit.**, p. 153
10. C. A. Evans, who secured the information from Chester Griffith, supplied the information by interview.
11. Mrs. May Dieckmann Stone, grandmother of Irene Sonnemann Beckwith, provided the information by interview.
12. C. A. Evans supplied the information by interview.
13. **Ibid.**
14. Burtschi, **op. cit.**, p. 21
15. John M. Heller related the incident while dining with the author in the room where the mural hangs.
16. Baringer, **op. cit.**, p. 4

ACKNOWLEDGEMENTS

The author is indebted to many persons who encouraged her in this undertaking. Her father taught her to investigate and then to cherish the Vandalia chronicles. Professor John T. Flanagan first introduced her to the study of Midwestern literature; his enthusiasm for the subject widened her interest and aided in leading her to the present research. The late Harry and his widow, Marian Pratt lent encouragement to the undertaking by their assistance in finding materials and by their gifts of significant volumes. Dr. A. W. Anderson read the manuscript and made valuable suggestions. Pauline Denton, Sandra Winslow, Susan Froehly, and Richard Strobel also made useful suggestions after reading the manuscript. The author is indebted to the staffs of the Evans Library, the main and architecture libraries and the Illinois Historical Survey at the University of Illinois, and the Illinois State Historical Library at Springfield. To all these persons who aided in the research at these libraries the author expresses her gratitude. The author is particularly indebted to Mr. C. A. Evans, who helped to secure pertinent information. To all her many excellent instructors in grammar, high school, college, and the university she acknowledges her gratitude.

M. P. B.

A Vandalian by birth, she has been reared under the influence of a zealous historian, her father, who was a collector of old books, items and documents relating to the history of the capital period (1820-1839). After she had received her bachelor of arts degree from Webster College of St. Louis University, she decided to teach high school English. Her father early in her life had directed her attention to the fact that the manner of pioneer living did not discourage the production of literature in the settlement of early Illinois. From 1827-1833 James Hall, an early state treasurer, left his stamp upon the cultural growth of the Midwest by the publication of three books and the first literary magazine of Illinois—all printed while he lived in Vandalia. After she had enrolled for the study of Middle Western literature in Dr. John T. Flanagan's course at the University of Illinois, she chose as her subject for special research the capital history of Vandalia, emphasizing James Hall's literary contributions.

Mary Burtschi, after receiving her master of arts degree from the University of Illinois in 1954, carried on her research for seven years. Dr. Robert M. Sutton, who generously encouraged her to complete her research, directed her to the Illinois Historical Survey, where she found valuable information. During the summer of 1961 she returned to the university where she pursued independent study by assembling her research into the present form. Since 1939 she has been a teacher of English in Effingham High School, Effingham, Illinois. At the present time besides being a teacher, she is president of the Vandalia Historical Society, a director in the Effingham Regional Historical Society, and a member of the Literary Landmarks committee of the Illinois Association of Teachers of English.

INDEX

INDEX